Notes From the Wild

The Nature Recording

Expeditions of

Bernie Krause

by
Bernie Krause

ellipsis arts...

Recordings & Text
Bernie Krause

Editor
Matthew Kopka

Art Direction/Design
Joanna Jaeger

Illustrations
Jerry Dadds

Executive Producer
Jeffrey Charno

For information or a catalog:
ELLIPSIS ARTS...
P.O. Box 305
Roslyn, NY 11576
P: 516-621-2727 F: 516-621-2750
E-MAIL:elliarts@aol.com

©1996 Ellipsis Arts...All Rights Reserved
No part of this book may be used or reproduced in any manner whatsoever without permission except in the case of brief quotations embodied in critical articles and reviews.

This album is dedicated to Manny Greenhill, who didn't live quite long enough for me to give him a hug for starting me on my way, and to my wife, Katherine, who continues to guide.

Table of Contents

Foreword by Jean-Michel Cousteau 5
Introduction 7
Suddenly, A New Sound from Heaven 10
Songs Our Fathers Sang 17
Transformations 23
Revelations 26
Notes From the Wild 30
    Amazon Nights......................................31
    Desert Solitudes 34
    A Gift from the Sea 38
    Whales, Wolves and Eagles of Glacier Bay 41
    Gorillas in the Midst..............................44
    Green Meadow Stream 51
Humphrey: The Rescue 53
A Higher Kinship 78
Notes from the Studio 83
Acknowledgments 90
Bernie Krause: Discography 91
Public Space Installations 93
Notes 94

CD Track Listing 95

Foreword

If a picture is worth a thousand words, what is a sound recording worth? Perhaps much more. With our eyes closed, we break free of two-dimensional thought, and become aware of nature in depth, to the sides and behind us, over our heads and even beneath our feet. A sound gives us more than a sensation of place—it triggers feelings of excitement or fear, commands our attention, awakens memories, makes us instantly and completely alert. When we listen to the sounds of nature, we are communicating with our aboriginal past on a level we may not entirely understand. It can be exhilarating or disturbing, but it never fails to touch us deeply. Listening to species like humpback whales or coyotes gives us a feeling of kinship with these creatures, and inspires the desire to protect them from extinction.

My friend Bernie Krause knows all these things, and for years he has been expanding the range of what we hear when we listen to the natural world. He also knows how much fun collecting sounds can be. Working together on the music video "Jungle Shoes" was more like play than labor, and the final product teaches us all that the world we live in, despite its hardships, remains the grandest playground we could ever hope for. And that preserving the world also means preserving a certain wondrous playfulness in ourselves.

Bernie's life and work are an amazing journey, one we can't afford to take for granted. We say we want peace and quiet, but Bernie knows better. What we really want is something worth listening to. There is plenty of it out there. Nobody knows how to find it better than Bernie Krause.

—*Jean-Michel Cousteau*

Introduction

"...The entity's life will be tempered with song, music, those things having to do with nature."
—*Edgar Cayce, from a "life reading" given when I was six weeks old.*

June 29, 1996

My parents hated animals. The few dogs and cats that made it across the threshold of our home never lasted very long. Usually, they were given away after just a few days. Caged creatures like hamsters were tolerated, but just barely. To my parents, animals fell into one or more of three categories: obviously dangerous, unclean, or—in some cases—edible. While this early influence failed to stem my curiosity about wildlife, it took some time before I was prepared to challenge the creature fear I learned at home.

Thankfully, however, my parents *did* love music. From earliest childhood the world of sound has been central to my life. Poor eyesight may partly explain the role it assumed for me. But my parents encouraged my interest, taking me with them to hear live performances when I was three years old. Half a year later I began to study violin, and by four, classical composition. I continued performing and composing with a variety of traditional stringed instruments well into the 1950s.

By the time I was ready for college my favorite instrument was the guitar; yet not a single music school I applied to in 1955 was prepared to accept me as a student with that as my principal instrument! In fact, after I had played a Bach Prelude perfectly during an audition, the Dean of Music at the University of Michigan exclaimed in a theatrical rage, "The guitar is *not* a musical instrument!" Out of despair, I became a crypto-guitarist, lurking behind a major in history.

Despite this, I continued to play guitar and to perform whenever I got the chance. In the meantime, the performance world of the 1950s and 60s underwent a shift from acoustic to electronic technologies, and my developing professional life as a musician paralleled those changes. I worked as a guitarist, performing on jazz and early Motown sessions, as a recording engineer and producer in an Ann Arbor recording studio, then as Pete Seeger's replacement—lead tenor and instrumentalist—in The Weavers[1] during their last year together.

Shortly after The Weavers' breakup I moved to California, to study electronic music at Mills College in Oakland. It was a time when avant garde composers like Karleinz Stockhausen and Pauline Oliveros were lecturing or passing through, demonstrating how to cut and assemble pieces of audio tape into coherent compositions. It was also the beginning of early experiments with modular synthesizers like the Buchla and Moog.[2]

During this period I met my partner, Paul Beaver[3], and formed a partnership—Beaver & Krause—that introduced the synthesizer to many well-known artists of the time; we also produced five albums of our own, and scored such feature films as *Rosemary's Baby*, *Apocalypse Now*, *Invasion of the Body Snatchers* and *Performance*, as well as TV shows like *Mission Impossible*, *The Twilight Zone* and *Bewitched*.

The allure of such projects wore off fairly quickly, however, and I became drawn to the world of natural sound. In 1979, at the age of 40, I enrolled in a doctoral program, and three years later completed a degree in Creative

Arts with an internship in bio-acoustics. As a naturalist, field recordist, sound sculptor and designer, I was at last combining my love of nature with my interest in sound, transforming authentic creature voices into recorded performances that represented both marine and terrestrial environments. For the past 28 years I have traveled the world, collecting sounds from every habitat that I have been able to reach. I cannot imagine a happier life.

In the pages that follow, I offer some observations on the wonders of natural sound, a few excerpts from my journals written while working in the field, and notes on the art and craft of bringing environments to life on CD, in the classroom and for public spaces. The enclosed CD will help illuminate these thoughts with examples from a number of habitats.

It's my hope that the book and recordings will inspire you to listen to the creatures of the natural world in new ways, and to actively conserve these precious voices for our children and the generations to come.

Suddenly A New Sound From Heaven

When we experience sound in the wilderness, all of our senses come into play. The irony, however, is that we tend to hear what we *see*. Standing by the seashore, we watch water lap at our feet, and hear millions of bubbles fizzle in the sand. The surge, curl and crash of the breakers draws our aural attention off with them, and we no longer hear the bubbles' chatter. Peering further down the beach, we hear the ocean's thunder, and quickly lose awareness of all "near-field" occurrences. Our hearing is further enhanced by what we feel on the surface of our skin, and even by smells around us.

Some of my more poetic colleagues refer to natural sound recording as *metaphor* or *illusion*. When I'm at work in the field, I'm always aware of this—I know that even my best recordings represent only *consequences* of sound.

Instinctively, we recognize the voices around us by the effects they create. When our eardrums vibrate, or the electromechanical membrane of a microphone responds to the complex wave forms made by an insect or bird, what we hear is a result of that particular *iteration* of our environment.

Over years of recording and replaying such sounds, I've learned that I can't simply go to the beach and record waves; technology won't allow it. As Gregory Bateson once observed, "The map is not the territory"; neither do raw recordings of forests or oceans become reality or even a beautiful replication untransformed. Our ears and collateral senses are miraculous; the technologies with which we record, reproduce and deliver sound are not. To accomplish the illusion of a moment at the seaside, the best audio naturalists must meaningfully reconstruct the experience.

In the mid-sixties I teamed up with Paul Beaver, a studio musician famous for his electronic effects and music contributions to film. Together we played a major role in introducing the synthesizer to the worlds of pop music, the broadcast media and film. We had already completed a major compositional work for Nonesuch Records called *The Nonesuch Guide to Electronic Music*, which described the fundamentals of acoustics and sound and became a standard reference in the field. Soon—before we had even released an album of our own—we were asked to duplicate effects we had created for Stevie Wonder, George Harrison, The Doors, The Byrds and other groups, as well as for many feature films. But we were restless, and eager to expand the art of the synthesizer to new areas.

We were sitting in our Los Angeles studio one fall day in 1968 when composer/songwriter Van Dyke Parks, who made his reputation in part as a collaborator with the Beach Boys, came by for a visit. Paul and I had been talking about a theme for our new album, and told Van Dyke that we were growing bored with continually replicating sounds we had long since mastered.

Van Dyke suggested we do something on *ecology*. It was a fresh word to us, but it would soon become familiar. With all of the emerging recording technologies, he suggested, it might be possible to record amazing things on location in the wild. We might even use natural sound as an element of composition, and at the same time address the need to save habitats through our music. At first, I confess, I wasn't so intrigued; Paul and I had always lived in cities and knew nothing about field recording, beyond the bit of ambient audio work we'd done for film.

But a spark was kindled. Paul had a small Uher portable tape recorder and a pair of decent mikes *(mics)*; I took them home and began to experiment. Meanwhile, we decided our album would be called *In a Wild Sanctuary*, a title taken from a then-current book by William Harrison about the wonders of the natural world.

But my first attempts to record in the field were not successful; we didn't know what to record or how to find it. Everywhere we went we encountered human-produced noise which masked many of the sounds we hoped to record. It didn't take us long to absorb the first rule of our work—find truly quiet places where there's no interference.

First I went alone to Muir Woods, the beautiful primary redwood forest north of San Francisco, in Marin County. There, aside from the occasional noise of circling light aircraft and distant traffic, I had my first experience with near-silence. It never occurred to me at the time that forests, especially California redwood forests, are relatively silent in late fall: the birds have nested and mated and the fledglings have long since gone, while insects and other creatures are absent or silent.

The exhilaration I felt the first time I heard the amplified sound of that place through my headphones, despite the relative lack of bird sound, was extraordinary! There was an immediate and palpable feeling of enormous space I'd been unaware of while listening with my ears alone—the microphones picked up many subtle sounds across far greater distances than my ears could.

I continued the search. I went to the ocean and recorded waves, visited a stream to record trickling water, walked to the beach by San Francisco's busy Fisherman's Wharf and—unaware of the controversies that would later develop about featuring human sounds as a part of wilderness recordings—attempted to capture people playing at the water's edge. I even tried the zoo.

Hearing the material at each site in stereo as I recorded it affected me powerfully. But when I returned to my studio and tried to play back my recordings, I was disappointed. None of the tracks sounded like they had when I captured them. The ocean waves sounded far away and compressed; the stream was little more than a flow of static; the redwood forest tape contained only hiss and some distant bird calls. Except for the sounds at Fisherman's Wharf, where I had somehow been fortunate, nothing sounded like I'd imagined it might. The magic of the places was lost, and I had no idea why.

We needed a stream for the album, but couldn't figure out how to make it "authentic." We tested many sites—streams as well as big bodies of flowing water. When we brought the recordings back and played them, none of them worked. Because Beaver and I had created numerous effects for films, we finally fell back on craft to achieve our aims. With no immediate alternative available, the stream sound on *In a Wild Sanctuary* was created by placing two microphones in a toilet bowl, adjusting the valve so that

water slowly trickled into the tank and finding the right position for the mikes.

We never got the ocean waves right; we synthesized them, as we did the storm sequence that one of the pieces called for. Conceptually, the album changed to reflect what the world would sound like after our natural environments were gone, when such sound would have to be synthesized anyway. But from that point on, we determined, we would never compromise again. Any natural sound we used would be recorded in the wild, and accurately reproduce the experience of being there.

I kept experimenting with site recordings. Late one evening, I found myself walking through the Nob Hill district in San Francisco, hunting for urban sounds that might inspire music. The rhythmic pulse of the streetcar cable, dragging beneath the road bed, caught my attention. As I crossed to the middle of the street to place my mikes in the cable slots, a fellow sauntered up to ask what I was doing. This curious man turned out to be Frank Oppenheimer, the brother of physicist J. Robert Oppenheimer who worked on the Manhattan Project, himself a physicist and teacher and founder of one of the country's first hands-on children's science museums, the Exploratorium. He was a short man with thinning hair and a weathered face lined from sun and academic pressures. Even on the dimly-lit street, his eyes flickered with interest as I explained my task.

We gathered some cable recordings, then went to a coffee shop. He coughed and chain-smoked, and we talked animatedly of the ways in which natural sounds—not to mention whole environments—were disappearing. I described our idea of recreating natural settings through sound performance pieces that conveyed the drama of such places. I suggested designing a piece for his museum.

Though he couldn't act on it, Oppenheimer liked the idea. "The sounds of pure nature are so rare now that people don't recognize them when they hear them," he said. "We've lost one of our most valuable assets." He said he'd had his own ideas about creating exhibits to demonstrate this devastation, but that they'd fallen on deaf ears. He hoped we would be more successful. (As it turned out, we were. Museum, zoo and aquarium installations are now a major part of the work done by my creative group, Wild Sanctuary.)

The album was finished in the spring of 1969. Our rendition of "Walking Green Algae Blues," featuring the late jazz and studio guitarist Howard Roberts and Paul on Hammond organ, is an environmental lament dedicated to Oppenheimer. Like other songs on the album, it contained both an anti-war and pro-environment message.

The album featured many innovations in music synthesis. It was the first time, for example, that natural sound was included as a component of orchestration in Western music.[4] Another first occurred on a tune called "Spaced," where we began by simulating wind chimes on the synthesizer, then took a single note—heard for the first time in the middle distance—and split it into eight separate notes. Four of these notes went up and four descended, in a forty-second glide from dissonance and chaos to full-chord resolution. That piece was copied by radio stations for their IDs, by an automobile company for its commercials and by an established northern California film company.

Historically, the album also preceded eco-musical efforts by Paul Winter and Judy Collins by at least seven years. Last but not least, *In a Wild Sanctuary* was the first music album encoded in both quadraphonic and surround sound!

I only found out later, while on a trip to Lausanne, Switzerland in the early 1970s, that Daniel Cohen-Bendit, the leader of the 1968 French student uprising, had adopted

"Walking Green Algae Blues" as the anthem of the German Green Party he was then forming. When I met him at my friend's apartment he was living "underground," using the place as a safe house. His writings on the need for clean air, safe water and recycling had stirred so much anger that someone had threatened his life.

In a Wild Sanctuary was an enormous critical success, though not a commercial one. Still, offers of film and studio work poured in from Hollywood, New York and London. In the meantime, however, I had discovered an exhilaration in outdoor work that I'd never known before, and began resenting time I spent cooped up in offices and studios. I was also growing tired of musician's jokes and life styles (a particular drug-filled session while working on The Doors' *Strange Days* album comes to mind: I watched in amazement as the music deteriorated and the night dragged on, with thousands of dollars literally going up in smoke). I began to find excuses to work where the air was fresh and I could learn a new craft. I didn't know it at the time, but I was on the path to becoming a naturalist.

Songs Our Fathers Sang

In 1969, a friend who had been studying Native American history gave me a book about the Nez Perce tribe. It included the speeches of Chief Joseph, a figure remembered for his eloquent defenses of tribal liberty in the face of late nineteenth century government oppression. I became curious about the very different accounts—from military journals, from interviews with Joseph, and from U.S. Army enlisted men and civilian witnesses—of what had taken place in the tribe's clashes with government forces. And I was intrigued by references in Joseph's speeches to his people's relationship to the environment.

This last theme in particular made me wonder if I could find some way to work with the tribe. With no specific plan, I found myself on an adventure that spanned several years.

Making contact with the tribe wasn't easy. Members I approached were suspicious, as were academics. Telephone calls weren't returned; letters went unanswered. But I kept trying to make some connection, and studied every piece of literature I could get my hands on, especially details of the tribe's 1,700 mile march from northeast Oregon in 1877, which led to Joseph's defeat and capture near Montana's Bear Paw Mountains by General O. O. Howard and several army regiments that Joseph had outfought for months. (The remnants of Joseph's band were exiled and not allowed to return to their traditional encampments. However, white families that have worked in Oregon for over a century, logging and mining until all the resources are nearly depleted, have recently invited the tribe back, mostly as a tourist attraction.)

When I finally arranged a visit to the reservation in Idaho, my difficulties were just beginning. I'd offered to help the tribal council to archive the Nez Perce language, and to create an aural repository of its songs and stories, but there had been little interest. My contacts within the tribe were few.

I brought along a colleague, Robert Primes, a cinematographer and director who had knowledge of film sound equipment and field recording; I didn't feel I could afford to make mistakes.

At first the tribe offered scant encouragement. Enough whites had ripped them off through the years; they weren't eager for more. Finally, I was introduced to Elizabeth Wilson. A tribal elder already in her 90s, Elizabeth appreciated our sincerity, and seemed eager to have her story recorded for posterity. She freely offered her songs, stories and sharp historical and social insights about both Indian religion and Christian missionaries' impact on tribal culture.

Though she was ailing and moved slowly, Elizabeth's wrinkled face spoke volumes about what she'd endured. Every time we visited her small log cabin near Kamiah she met us at the door, her head wrapped in a bandanna, in cotton print dresses we learned she had made for herself, starting to speak long before we were able to set up our mikes and tape recorders.

It turned out that at her 1904 graduation from the Carlisle Indian School in Pennsylvania, Elizabeth had met Chief Joseph and General Howard, both of whom had been asked to give commencement speeches.[5] Because Elizabeth knew "the genteel and civilized Western tool of shorthand," as she called it, she copied and translated Joseph's speech, which was to be his last. He died a few months later.

Later, Elizabeth introduced us to a group of native singers and drummers, all in their 70s and 80s, who had been part of a musicians' assembly that formed in the early 1920s. The introduction was sufficient to establish trust between us, and they invited us to record their drumming and singing.

The trip yielded a lesson about music I could never have learned in school. After some weeks on the reservation, Elizabeth's son Angus, then in his mid-70s, urged us to go with him to Lake Wallowa—hallowed ground for the Nez

Perce and Joseph's band in northeast Oregon. Angus had described several sites where we might record the birds, streams and breezes of the late October fall.

Joseph's father was buried at the north end of the lake, and the surrounding land was sacred to the group—the reason, I suppose, why Angus took us there. Even in the early 70s, though, there were ominous signs of change. Condos and homes were being built all around the shoreline. Marinas and boat ramps were being constructed at every possible site. The great pine forests that once surrounded the lake were already clear-cut far back into the mountains, with picnic benches springing up along the lake's few feeder streams in alarming numbers. Still, there remained a few untouched spots, and Angus took us to one of them.

"You boys think you know something about music?" he asked. "You don't know nothing. Let me show you. Sit here by this stream and be quiet."

We sat for ten minutes. Then we sat for twenty. Angus, who was 50 feet away, stared at the stream, oblivious to our presence. It was a bitter-cold morning and ice was everywhere, especially where we sat huddled on the ground.

The longer we sat the colder we got, until finally, just when I thought I'd had enough of our wilderness adventure, a breeze from the valley above us began to whistle through the branches of the aspens. Suddenly, to our surprise, there arose the sound of a huge pipe organ!

Primes and I looked at each other to be sure we weren't hallucinating. At that moment Angus stirred, looked in our direction, got up and came over to us. Seeing the look of wonder on our faces, he asked if we knew the sounds' origin. We shook our heads no.

Angus walked over to the stream, and with his knife, cut off one of the reeds that stood by the shore. He brought it back, covered one end with his hand, then blew into the other, creating a long, low tone. He pointed to the different length reeds along the stream bed and said, "See what the wind does? That's how we got our music, and that's how you got yours. But you have forgotten." With his knife, he cut holes in the reed and began to play. We recorded him as he tested the instrument, and with his permission, used the performance in a piece featuring stories by Elizabeth Wilson called *"Legend Days Are Over"* which appears on *All Good Men*, the last album Paul Beaver and I did for Warner Brothers (1973).

From that cold October morning by a stream in once-sacred country, my beliefs about the origins of our music and environment began to change. On "Legend Days," Elizabeth tells the following story about her world and its destruction:

> *The way the medicine men went and got guiding spirit — contact with animals or whatever it is — they kept on dancing every winter. They got strong and power came to them. Power came to them.*
>
> *Everything was different. It must have been in those times when everything was different. Clear air and wilderness, and they could get in touch with animals like that. But I don't think they can now. Everything gone, noise and all.*
>
> *All right! Legend days will be over; humanity is coming soon. No more legend days. There will be no more. And they will be sad like I am, brokenhearted over my last child, never to return again. Death takes her. And that's the way it's going to be.*
>
> *I wander along only in the higher mountains, and the heads of the streams all the way through. I'm never down anywhere where it's civilized country — I'm way up in the wilderness. Years to come people will lose their only child*

and they'll have the feeling just like I have: sad. And that's why these days we are that way. Sadness comes to us.

Elizabeth died a year after the album's release, but not before I played her the recording. "I didn't know I said all those things!" she told me.

In the wake of such epiphanies, I began spending every moment I could away from studios and film sets, out in the field, searching for new places to record.

I had become addicted to the natural world.

Transformations

By the late 1970s, I had come to a real crossroads. I was frustrated working indoors, and longing for a complete change in my life.

But where could I go, for what purpose? Taking refuge in madness was one option; religion was another. I was considering these alternatives one summer's evening while camping alone in the "slick rock" country of southern Utah, where the rock surfaces have been worn thin by the wind and desert sands, when the repeated lone note of a cricket, rubbing its delicate wings together, caught my attention—the beautiful rasp seemed to fill the desert stillness. "The heartbeat of the high desert," I thought, and jumped up, eager to find a way to capture the moment and its impact with the recording equipment in my backpack. I wanted to secure the pulsing voice on audio tape, to play its song whenever my peace was disturbed.

The problem, as I'd soon discover, was that natural environments and creatures hold secrets they're slow to reveal. How to faithfully shift that solitary cricket's voice from its home in the rocks to a medium like a compact disc is an enigma that continues to haunt me.

But I was on my way. Over the next fifteen years I became consumed with a desire to record in natural environments and to preserve the sounds of native habitats, spending as much as seven months out of each year in the field. My journeys took me from pole to pole, to many equatorial sites and to hundreds of locations in-between. I worked at Gombe, Dr. Jane Goodall's Tanzanian reserve, recording her research chimpanzees; at Karisoke, the late Dian Fosse's mountain gorilla site in Rwanda's Virunga Mountains; and at Birute Galdikas' Camp Leakey in Borneo, where she and her team rehabilitate former captive orangutans in an attempt to reintroduce them to Indonesia's dwindling tropical forests. I have also recorded many different species of whales, from the north slope of Alaska to the Antarctic, harvester ants as close to home as my backyard, and — in a ditch by the road not far from where I live — insect larvae in vernal pools created by a late spring downpour.

The path wasn't always clear, and there have been distractions. Environmental paradigms of the 1960s, 70s and 80s, for example, reinforced the *separation* between humans and the natural world. "Let's keep it pure," came the decrees from every so-called "green" corporate headquarters. As late as 1989, a national company selling nature-related products ordered me to take the sound of human footsteps out of an album I made with a colleague. On that album, we needed the cadence of footsteps to convey a sense of the rhythm of a walking journey along the "Good Red Road," the mystical route a number of Native American tribes traversed on vision quests through the high deserts of the West, a sacred path across North America.

"Keep the human elements out of Nature," we were informed. "Our clients won't understand what humans were doing there." The marketing department wanted to keep out of our work what we knew to be absolutely germane to it. We were already pairing human-produced *music* with nature sounds on many albums — why not include sounds of humans interacting in positive and natural ways with their environment? They were never able to explain the paradox to us, other than to say that the combination of music with nature sounds helped sales.

Sad to say, the romantic paradigm of "nature," separate from human beings, still holds strong. Corporate mandates of this type exist even now in the best-intentioned circles. When we delivered a Christmas album done with animal sounds to one corporate entity, we were told that the mandate *du jour* was "no domestic animals."

"But—" I told the executive who delivered this news, "I just bought a tote bag from your store, and it's made of leather."

"It's dead," came the rejoinder. To which I couldn't help retorting, "Well so are the animals on my album. After we recorded them, we ate 'em!"

The word "nature" itself, employed with hollow reverence, too often separates us from that to which we are most inextricably linked. None of the 500 original Native American languages had a single word for "nature." These folks didn't see themselves as being detached.

Revelations

One of my most important insights came in February 1983, while on a field trip sponsored by the California Academy of Sciences to record natural sounds in Kenya. I'd been working for several weeks in the high African plains when late one evening by a waterhole in the Aberdare Salient, I realized that the din generated by the millions of night creatures around me wasn't noise at all. Instead, those organisms were creating a distinctive orchestration. Although I could distinguish one animal voice from another, they seemed to be performing together as a body of instruments, just like those in a contemporary musical orchestra: crickets in one niche, cicadas and other insects in another. Frogs in their niche. Birds in theirs. *Music!*

The moment I got home, I rushed to the lab, booted up the computer, and created a graphic demonstration of what I had heard. As these *spectrograms*, or voice prints, were transformed on the screen into related patterns, I knew I had discovered evidence of important ties. Before me was a graphic illustration of the sound of that African night. On it, those creatures' voices looked like an avant-garde musical score, one that could have been created by John Cage or Pierre Boulez. The notation was so distinct that it might have been recreated and read as an orchestration for synthesizer or computer! But though I recognized meaningful connections, there were still missing pieces.

A possible further link occurred to me some time later, while working with a group of hunter-gatherers called the Jivaro in the western Amazon. At the suggestion of a colleague, I had visited them to record the ambience of their forest habitat. It didn't occur to me at the time to record their music as well. I realize now that I overlooked an opportunity, because what I *heard* in their music was an impressive link to the sounds of the rain forest. Their music, in fact, sprang directly from the insect, frog and bird sounds that surrounded them. I was too stubborn to appreciate what I was hearing. While I have not had an opportunity to return and record that area and its people, this idea continues to intrigue me.

In the past several years, other evidence connecting the music of hunter-gatherers with their surroundings—an idea I have come to call "the niche hypothesis"—has presented itself. The New Guinea recordings of Steven Feld of the University of California in Santa Cruz, and the incredible recordings of Louis Sarno, who has done such extraordinary work with the Bayaka pygmies of the Central African Republic, add weight to the idea. The work of these two men demonstrates a special appreciation for the rare points where humans and their natural circumstances still intersect.

The influence of natural sound on some cultures goes beyond language and music. Some cultures even map their territory by it. In July 1989, while recording north of Daintree in northeast Australia, I happened to run across Simon Fell, an ecologist who works in the field of sustainable agriculture. After dinner in our forest lodgings beside a river, he recounted some of his experiences with the Pitjantjara, a nomadic central Australian aboriginal tribe.

"The Pitjantjara have sixteen different time concepts," Fell told me. "They have a circular time concept in which events of particular importance to the culture repeat themselves.

They have springtime concepts, where events repeat themselves over time, transforming the natural elements in their environment both physically *and* spiritually. And they have still other spring concepts where incidents repeat with increasing frequency, culminating in an important ceremonial event. One example of this is the *corroboree*, or dance festival, an event that arouses great excitement among them. As the date grows closer it is talked about with greater frequency, until the festival eventually takes place.

"The Pitjantjara also have 'no-time' or non-linear time concepts," Fell told me, "and dream-time, which is what a lot of Western people have latched onto recently, because it's fairly easy to comprehend. Dream-time is actually a form of no-time concept, filled with creation myths that have no conceptual beginning or end. In total, the Pitjantjara seem to have sixteen distinctly different notions of time based on very sophisticated metaphysical systems.

"These notions of time consume much of the Pitjantjara's thought, and help define their lives. But subtle definitions of sound in their environment play an almost equally important role. One group member, for example, will often describe a distant meeting place to another almost completely by acoustic clues. They speak in great detail, mind you, of what would appear to us an immense habitat of flat, dry, featureless landscapes, where we would find almost nothing to distinguish one location from another. Parts of Australia are filled with open spaces like these, and it isn't as if there are obvious geological features there—to the Pitjantjara, it is the combined acoustic effect of small local plants and animals that serves as a guide. Sound is one of the most important features they isolate as part of their *holographic* map, the three-dimensional map of the world as it manifests in their minds.

"As members of the Pitjantjara travel either alone or in

small groups from semi-arid to arid country, they identify the species of animals that range through the *biomes* (distinct habitats) they traverse. They have also learned that the syntax, timbre, frequency and duration of those animals' vocalizations have evolved to match subtle geographic and climactic variations in their habitats. These vocal differences serve as beacons to them as they travel through the desert.

"One person is able to describe those differences in the form of sound contours to a fellow traveler, thereby providing a fix on a location. The Pitjantjara's language is filled with descriptive dialogue that binds them to their environment. I've traveled with them, and I find their land-navigational abilities amazing!

"Sound is but one of several distinctions the Pitjantjara employ to describe locations; color is another. A certain species of copperhead snake, for example, has markings that get lighter the further north it lives. The leaf shape of a species of desert bush will change as you travel from a semi-arid to an arid region. When all of the contours of the described sonic and visual features converge, you have arrived.

"It would be extremely difficult for us to learn more than a fraction of what the Pitjantjara know about such things in an entire lifetime. When I asked them whether this knowledge was a gift from the gods, they were quite offended, and shunned me for a time. It's clearly not an esoteric thing to them. Scholarship is an intrinsic part of their education, and each of them works damned hard to learn what they know. It became clear to me that the Pitjantjara knew what a highly developed art they had, and that they wanted more recognition for it, rather than to have others think that it just landed in their laps by divine grace."

Notes From the Wild

The six selections that follow were all taken from rare habitats, magical places where one can still go to experience the peace that inspires—locations where once, very long ago, we took our place as just one of many voices in God's choir. The descriptions do not always relate directly to the recordings on the CD; instead, they represent experiences at the sites, which include a lush tropical rainforest, a fragile desert in the American Southwest, a mid-ocean reef, a pristine spot in southeast Alaska, the Virunga Mountains of Rwanda where the mountain gorillas live, and a mountain stream. Each of these locations demonstrates a unique orchestral balance between its players. Each of these places has, at one time or another, impelled mortals to create music. Most of these recordings were made either very late at night or in the earliest hours of the morning.

(CD Track 1)
Amazon Nights

February 10, 1990
Kilometer 41 research camp,
north of Manaus, Brazil.

In the jungle tonight, while my colleague Ruth Happel and I were recording, we smelled the unmistakable scent of a nearby jaguar. We were alone in the forest several kilometers from camp where there was no moon or other light apart from the beams of our flashlights. We never saw or heard the animal but knew it was close by, perhaps just a few feet away.

Our senses were certainly *heightened*, but I don't believe either of us sensed that we were in immediate danger. Sitting quietly about 50 meters apart, we recorded for an hour. Then, around midnight, Ruth went down the trail in one direction and I went off in another, to try to collect the widest possible variety of night sounds.

After I had been walking for about fifteen minutes, I sat down alone beside the trail and began to record. Only then did I hear the cat's low snarl in my headphones. It must have been following me, but nothing I heard before the growl suggested it had come so close. The sound of its breath in my earphones indicated the cat was probably not more than a couple of feet from the microphone tripod I had set up 30 feet down the trail. My heart skipped several beats but I remained still, clutching my recorder with a grip not usually recommended for very sensitive equipment. If the recorder had been anything but a very sturdy Nagra, it would have been twisted beyond recognition! I managed to record some low growls and breaths from the creature, which indicated it was sniffing the microphone, although I couldn't see what was happening in the dark and had no

intention of startling it with my flashlight. An event that lasted no more than a minute seemed like a couple of hours as I sat there, mesmerized by the power of the animal's voice, breath and the sounds of rumbles in its stomach. Then, as suddenly as it appeared, the cat moved silently off into the forest, leaving only the throbbing pulse of frogs and insects in the night.

We returned to camp about an hour ago (3:00 AM), and I still can't sleep. Although I'm dead tired—we got up to record the dawn chorus 24 hours ago—I can't take in enough of the incredible sounds this forest performs. There is such precision and richness in the insect and frog orchestration, such a tight fit of creature harmonies, I'm beginning to feel that Western music often pales by comparison. The howler monkeys put their vocal stamp on the proceedings with a deep-throated roar that can be heard for miles throughout the canopy above us. There's a sense of safety and peacefulness I've never known before.

This morning at breakfast we told the guides and the cook about our recording, and played them the sounds of the jaguar through our earphones. The camp cook began to joke about some of the prior visitors this camp has seen. He told of an American actor who claimed to be an environmentalist, who had visited the camp a few months before. The way the cook told it, this Hollywood top gun came with a retinue of twenty or so people, bodyguards and photographers who never left his side, not even when he went to relieve himself. He seemed afraid to venture more than 100 meters from camp, even with his guides and armed guards. Apparently he didn't stay long, because his bodyguards complained the hammocks and food weren't as commodious as the beds and fine meals in the fancy hotel in Manaus. To retain some credibility, they took a few photos in the forest near camp and left. The cook found the whole thing funny. Later, he took me aside to ask why this fellow was so important. I was at a loss for words.

On the way back to Manaus from camp, we passed over logging roads cut through the forest. They were muddy, and so deeply rutted that our truck, which is high-centered, maneuvered over them only with great difficulty. Along much of the course, barren stretches of land peppered with stumps where trees once stood lay exposed to the equatorial sun, the red clay sculpted into arroyos by erosion. A few houses dotted this moonscape, and we stopped at one to pick up a passenger. He told us that his family moved to this place from the forest two years ago, thinking that they could farm here. But the thin soil that supported a year's worth of crops is now gone, victim of erosion and nutrient depletion from exposure to the wind and rain. Soon the family will have to move again and clear more forest just to survive.

In Borneo, where I recently recorded orangutans for another project, the rainforest was once considered a source of unlimited wood and mineral supplies. In the past ten years, loggers and miners have destroyed what took millennia to create, including entire cultures who fought hard to preserve their ways. Often these unprotected groups fought with nothing more than blowpipes and poison arrows. The lives of Borneo's Penan forest people have been broken for scaffolding, chopsticks and paper products. The Penan's medicinal plants and food sources are decimated, and blackwater rivers that once ran clean look like milky tea. I sit here wondering what their music will be like when the animals that once inspired their melodies are gone.

(CD Track 2)

Desert Solitudes

Monday, April 27, 1992
*Gray Ranch, in the panhandle of New Mexico,
on the U. S. - Mexico border*

We have come to record the Chihuahua-Sonora desert, a transitional habitat consisting mostly of secondary growth. Until recently, it was populated almost entirely by domestic animals. Since the arrival of the Spanish nearly 500 years ago, the deserts of the Mexican north and American southwest have been host to the cattle, sheep, dogs and cats brought here by missionaries and their followers. The whole environment was transformed. Little by little, though, the pressure on this fragile habitat has diminished. The flora and fauna are beginning to return, but only because of the careful husbandry of The Nature Conservancy, which now controls the site. The ranch covers 500 square miles and, except for a few cattle and a small number of ranchers, we're alone.

For nearly a week we have been working tiny sections of this vast plot. Ruth Happel and I, on assignment to acoustically map sections of the ranch, remain utterly undisturbed by the outside world. We share the space with the wind, coyotes, meadowlarks, ravens, hawks, reptiles and a great number of other spring birds and insects. We've taken off our watches to better adjust to the desert's rhythms. Time passes quickly, anyway; there never seems to be enough of it. Our tape supply is short too; we hadn't planned for the acoustic riches this desert has chosen to reveal.

Most exciting, we have finally discovered a genuinely quiet place, one undisturbed by the noise of aircraft and automobiles. In ten days we've heard only one light aircraft overhead, and virtually no cars have gone past the ranch gates. During this time we've been acoustically mapping our temporary home, and have made a discovery. Within the five or so square miles we are working we have identified more than 50 micro-habitats, each quite distinct from the next. By their sound alone, certain insects and birds appear to establish very specific territories. The harmonious mix of creature voices marks the boundaries of each environment. We can define mini-habitats by the sound of certain creatures that live there and actually map such places with new rules. Our work is becoming truly driven by sound, which seems to suggest a whole new area of science. And we have determined how some very different creatures define their turf.

I sit here wondering how anyone could think that deserts are really *empty*. From 33,000 feet—passing over in a plane or rushing across it at 75 miles an hour on a ribbon of concrete, I guess—a desert might indeed seem dead. And it's true that the desert reveals its mysteries only to those with infinite patience—a skill we have had to learn, sitting in one place for many hours just to witness a single event, or to hear one sound. This afternoon, we caught sight of a rare aplomado falcon. Previously thought to be extinct here, it floated unconcerned on the desert thermals above our heads for many wonderful minutes. Later, when we stopped at ranch headquarters and told a biologist what we had seen, he said the falcon hadn't been observed here for years.

We set up camp for the night, commenting on how amazed we were by the life we have found and recorded here. Then, just before sundown, we recorded ants *singing!*

A vast number of red ants had been circling our campsite, moving ever closer to our food and tents. At one point we considered pouring a ring of gasoline around both to keep them at bay, but instead I dropped a little lapel microphone into the hole leading to their nest. A number of the creatures immediately began to gather, seemingly trying to find a way to remove it. At that point I switched on my recorder and discovered, much to our surprise, that they were emitting a plaintive, high-pitched sound, a kind of call-and-response. They were coordinating their movements through some kind of dialogue, we realized, trying to lift the microphone out of the hole!

Tuesday, April 28

The thunderstorm ended in the late afternoon, and was followed by a breeze. I haven't ever been able to get a good recording of wind, and at first it didn't occur to me to try. (What we really hear is the *effect* of wind, the tonal result of a strong gust as it travels through cracks in a wall, around a corner or over exposed splinters of wood on a windowpane or door.) Each time I tried, I overloaded the microphones—and got blasted—since the equipment has difficulty handling that kind of air pressure. This afternoon, however, I got another chance. I was sitting by a barbed wire fence when my ear caught the whistle of wind as it passed through the twists and barbs in a rusted wire filament just a few inches off the ground.

When I put my mikes close to the cable, the transducer was still getting overloaded. I carefully buried the mikes in the low-lying grass just below the most active wire, then turned on the recorder and waited about 50 feet away while the wind blew, the wire whistled, and the recorder did its magical work. The grass protected the microphones from direct contact with the wind and, except for the occasional song of a meadowlark, the recordings were splendid.

It's cold tonight, and I'm trying to stay warm. I've got my recorder ready in case the coyotes come near enough to sing for me. In the meantime I throw more mesquite on the fire and reach for a cup of cocoa that's been warming on the grate. A satellite moves slowly from north to south across the western sky. The pair of jackrabbits I've been watching since dusk has gotten bolder and are playing at the foot of my microphone tripod, within arms' reach. The beauty of the desert is so transparent it seems holy. I feel as near to God as I've ever felt before, and sense that if we shared a whole "earth of worship" instead of dwelling in separate "houses," our lives could be vastly improved.

(CD Track 3)

A Gift from the Sea

Pfeiffer Beach, California, February 1991;
Maui, Hawaii, February 1979;
The Great Barrier Reef, Australia, September 1989.

Above and below the ocean surface creatures vocalize, each signaling its part in the complex orchestration of sounds that signal the presence of life there. As in the rainforests, there are discernible and measurable patterns — strict rules of natural orchestration that, except during periods of ecological stress, don't usually vary. The creatures know the score. It'll probably take several generations before we have much of an idea about how the rules work, but we can be reasonably certain that any deviation from normal vocal or physical behavior by one creature means it might end up as another's meal! Instinctively, these creatures adjust to their habitats in ways we can only speculate on.

Once, when I was recording and researching humpback whale sounds off of Maui during the late 1970s, I decided to take a scuba break. I dove down to about 30 feet and hung there for some minutes. Out of the gloom, heading toward me at the same depth, came a large female humpback and her baby. I remained unmoving as 40 feet of whale approached, her pectoral fins spread wide as the wings of a small jet plane. The only problem was that her fins were on the same lateral plane as my throat! I remained frozen. At the very moment when a section of the animal's fin would have made contact with my Adam's apple, just that part of her arched, and glided millimeters over my head. I could feel the displacement of the water as she passed, but remained unscathed. My heart raced and I almost lost my breath, but I managed, slowly, to regain a sense of where I was. I had no idea just how sensitive these creatures were.

When we're doing aquatic work like recording whales, there are often intense periods of action. When I'm recording in the forest, however, while there is always *some* activity, long periods often pass while I simply sit and wait. Sometimes I'll remain quietly in one spot for 30 hours or more, just to get a sense of a habitat. Then something may happen and I might be lucky enough to have my tape recorder running. Sometimes I never get what I'm after. The sound I hear on one particular morning may not occur again for much longer periods than I can remain on site.

With sound we can illustrate both time or space, or recreate both. Presented on the enclosed CD is a journey from an ocean beach to a coral reef below the water's surface. The sounds occurring after the transition from the beach to the reef include several varieties of shore birds and fish, and two types of whales. The common names of some of them include: killdeer, California gulls, California sea lions, killer whales and humpback whales. The fish include the long horn sculpin, striped sea robin, file fish, black drum, Atlantic croaker, red drum, ocean triggerfish, puffer fish and snapping shrimp. As it turns out, there are nearly 200 species of fish that generate sound by gnashing their teeth, gnawing at coral or using their swim bladders. Even though I've become used to hearing them, their voices never lose their wonder for me.

Often, when I play these sounds while giving school

presentations, the notion of a fish making noise seems incomprehensible to students. It's always a stretch to get people to believe these are sounds that animals make. I've discovered a way, though. It can be done with music! About ten years ago, I grew frustrated trying to make presentations to students by just talking and playing a few recordings on cheap auditorium speakers. I couldn't hold their attention.

Then I hit on the idea of recording samples of fish sounds I had in my library that sounded like percussion instruments. Using drum fish that sound like a kick drum, parrot fish that sound like scraper (a grooved gourd), and snapping shrimp that sound like closed high-hat cymbals, I laid down several such tracks, creating a percussion ensemble. I added humpback whales to play the part of violins and guitars, depending on how they happened to vocalize. Walruses performed the "bass" and "cow bell." Chimps made up the sound of the piano. I put all of these animal sounds together and created an album called *Gorillas in the Mix*.

The next time I made a presentation, I installed a 200 watt rock and roll speaker system on the stage. I didn't say a word when I walked out in front of the audience. I cranked the volume to full, pushed the play button on my tape recorder, and let the music rip with a gorilla rap tune called "Ape No Mountain High Enough. " There was no way the kids could compete, and they stopped talking. When the tune finished I told them that all of the musical sounds were biological. Met with some skepticism, I offered them a deal. "Give me 20 minutes to prove the point and I'll play you another tune done the same way," I bargained. I'd found a way to deliver an important environmental message, and they had discovered a new way to listen to the natural world.

(CD Track 4)
Whales, Wolves and Eagles of Glacier Bay

I'm often asked what part of the world I like best. A more diplomatic person might say "Right here," and make his hosts happy, but of all the places I have traveled and recorded, Alaska is the most beautiful and compelling. To my mind, it's the last truly "wild" place left, in the nineteenth century American romantic sense of the word. The diversity of its geography and animal life is stunning. From the North Slope on the Beaufort Sea to Sitka in the southeast, there are countless major and micro-habitats including numerous mountain ranges, huge expanses of tundra, dry and wet sub-Arctic rainforests, islands and river environments, and only half a million residents.

For several years I worked and led listening expeditions, mostly of sea-going kayaks, just west of Juneau. During the summer of 1979, as part of a research project testing the relationship between the diminishing population of humpback whales in Glacier Bay and tourist vessel noise, I happened to witness a remarkable exchange between three killer whales and a humpback — the only one apparently not driven out of the Bay by the incredible noise that season. The excerpt from my journal reads:

August 1, 1979
Fingers Bay, just west of Willoughby Island

After two weeks on a research boat, I got up enough nerve to jump into the bay and wash off. For a body unused to 48 degree water, the shock was unforgettable — but not nearly as memorable as the glimpse I caught as I climbed back on board of three orca whales soundlessly diving under the hull not ten feet from where I'd just been swimming, and heading straight for a humpback feeding near the shore. I switched on the recorder just in time to catch their confrontation.

There were grunts and screams; then the humpback lunged. One killer whale leaped out of the water and came down with an astounding splash. The humpback slapped its tail in apparent alarm—like a cannon shot, it resonated and echoed right across the bay. The whole thing was over in a matter of minutes, and after a final burst of screams, the killer whales were seen moving south away from the humpback. For now, the animal is safe. But I've seen film of a killer whale pod attacking a very large blue whale; the damage these animals can inflict leaves an indelible impression.

June 1, 1992
Off of Point Adolphus on Chicagoff Island

The sea was incredibly calm today. I went out in a kayak with Nate Borson, and we drifted in the afternoon sun for close to an hour. For a long time we watched a young bald eagle learning to fish. Lacking the grace of adults, it swooped to the surface of the water, trying unsuccessfully to snag the plentiful salmon and dolly vardon that swam within reach. After many tries, it managed to hook a salmon in its talons, but the fish wiggled lose as the bird gained altitude.

Nate suggested we drop the hydrophone into the water. No sooner did the instrument reach enough depth to record when I heard, unimpeded by other vessel noise for the first time in the area, incredible humpback vocalizations. A pod of six animals was feeding not far from where we drifted. As we watched, the humpbacks dove to the bottom of Icy Straights. Then, swimming upward in an ascending spiral, they blew a ring of bubbles. The bubbles formed a kind of net, causing fish and tiny, shrimp-like krill to collect in a mass in the middle. All at once, the humpbacks lunged up from the depths through the bubble-net, scooping up great amounts of food in their maws, forcing the excess water out through their baleen with huge tongues and leaving the krill compressed in their mouths.

To witness this event is remarkable enough. But just then one of the animals let out a cry—a long, mid-range tone with a descending coda at the end. Fortunately, my recorder was switched on, and I caught the whole sequence of bubbles and vocalizations. It was the first time I or anyone else had ever managed to record this entire feeding succession of events without lapping waves or boat propellers jamming the transducer. I recorded their activity for about half an hour. It took fifteen years of work to capture the moment, but what splendid recordings we have!

At this writing, Alaska too is under siege. Pressure to open up new oil reserves and to cut down the temperate rainforests of the southeast is stronger than it's been in several decades. Industry must find ways to be gentler with these resources. If it can't, we will have to help them do it, through regulation and enforcement. Either way, the responsibility rests on us all to make do with much less. See Alaska if you can, then ask yourself—as your eyes feast on its incredible beauty and your lungs fill with the planet's freshest air—whether or not the place is worth conserving.

(CD Track 5)
Gorillas in the Midst

September 12, 1987
*From my journal while recording at Karisoke,
the late Dian Fosse's research station in the
Virunga Mountains of Rwanda*

Second day in the field. My legs felt heavy, powerless and sore. I had to learn to walk all over again, taking very high steps, otherwise my feet became tangled in the vines and nettles of the secondary growth of this sublimely magical forest. I couldn't keep my balance for more than a few strides without stumbling. Also, we're at about 8,000 feet, walking up and down a couple of thousand feet every few miles as we hike to locate the animals. After about three hours of pain, we located the group we were seeking. I was left alone while the other researchers and Nick Nichols, a *National Geographic* photographer, staked out positions among the gorillas.

Yesterday, I was introduced to Ziz, the group's dominant silverback male, and his young male rival, Pablo. As we approached the group's deep forest location today we heard screams from some kind of battle, although we had no idea who was fighting or why. By the time we arrived, it looked like a bomb had exploded—everything was uprooted and levelled. Pablo was sulking at a goodly distance from Ziz. He was sitting on his haunches, head buried in his hands, while the other gorillas munched on nearby vegetation. It's typical for males to fight over females; the dominant male always wins. I didn't realize until too late that I'd positioned myself between Pablo and Ziz; and I didn't realize the fight was not quite finished.

I had my recorder on, and was sitting with my back to Pablo when I heard a crash of vegetation. Because my mikes are stereo, I am only able to get a sense of the sound coming from either right or left; I had no way of knowing that the sound came from *directly* behind me. I discovered that fact when Pablo's forceful hand grabbed my right shoulder, picked me up— equipment and all—and flung me fifteen feet into a patch of stinging nettles!

I experienced several sensations while airborne. One of these was momentary weightlessness, which—considering the heavy weight of my equipment—I welcomed. I also experienced the incredible power of the mountain gorilla, particularly when it's upset. Other than the stinging nettles that brushed my face when I landed, I experienced no pain from the fall, only a profound sense of awe. Pablo was only clearing a path as he moved to attack Ziz once again. I happened to be one of several objects in the way. A couple of female gorillas got tossed as well.

September 19

Time spent in this forest is both rewarding and harrowing. Today was typical. While following Group Five we recorded a large range of vocalizations. At first the animals were very quiet, and hardly vocalized—I was beginning to think that nothing much would happen, but decided to wait a little while. The animals are now so used to me that I'm able to nest down with them during their noon siesta while waiting for the rains to stop. After a nap they're often very vocal, and I hope I'll be lucky. (While preparing for this trip, I listened to a few gorilla recordings Fosse made; I hope to add to the repertoire she began collecting.)

As soon as the rain stopped and they woke up, my patience paid off. Screams, grunts, sounds of playing, singing, fights, grooming and eating—all of the material I really need to create something great on tape materialized.

At one point around mid-afternoon, an enormous elephant emerged from the wall of green. The trackers were the first to see it, and they high-tailed it for a nearby *hygenia* tree, yelling "*Tembo! Tembo!*" (elephant in *ki-Swahili*). I was all settled in a comfortable position in an abandoned gorilla day nest, happily recording, when the elephant either caught our scent or saw us, and sounded a terrifying alarm. In the meantime, the gorilla group had split, and Nichols and Lorna Anness, a researcher from Scotland who joined us for the day, followed the trackers up the same convenient tree, leaving me out in the open, tangled in my equipment.

Everyone yelled at me to get out of the way! In the confusion I finally got myself together, along with my equipment, and scrambled to safety with the others. Now there were five of us hanging fourteen feet above the ground, dangerously perched on a single slender branch. The elephant's extended trunk came so close I could feel and smell its hot breath on my clammy skin. We must have been up there for some time; my ass became numb from straddling the branch. Finally, the elephant lumbered into the forest. After waiting for what seemed another eternity I descended, cautiously followed by Nick and Lorna. The porters didn't come down for another half an hour. They probably knew something we didn't.

October 2

Without much sleep we set off again, into the forest to follow the Beatsme group (Fosse assigned both numbers and names to each group, first naming each for its primary silverback) with Lorna. She and David Watts are the only two full-time Westerners in the camp. Nick went off to see Group 5 with David, and I'm hoping for an easier day. Our trackers told us that Beatsme's group is closer to camp than several of the others. We followed them just over the border into Zaire on a hike that was not quite as arduous as our mountain treks. Still, I'm tired, and ache all over from fatigue. I'm also irritated, because nothing dries here. My socks and shoes are always wet. We're running out of fresh food stock, and need to order more. Everyone else is so stalwart and forbearing that I keep my mouth shut and pretend to be intrepid, though I'm certain my body language belies my feelings.

We sat, watched and recorded the Beatsme group for two hours, taping non-stop. The animals weren't vocalizing much. The weather on our side of the mountain finally turned sunny and warm, and our clothes began to dry. Lorna and I sat there in the nettles and watched as the giant silverback hugged, groomed and played with his newborn offspring as well as a couple of juveniles and an immature female. We left the gorillas just as they rose from their midday nap, and began to head back to camp after connecting with the tracker and porter. As we began to pick up the trail, I said to Lorna, "I smell a silverback!" The smell is unmistakable—a combination of body sweat and strong herbs.

Not a moment later, there was a terrifying, earsplitting scream, and a lot of thrashing and chestbeating as the animal crashed through the undergrowth toward us. Apparently, Beatsme sighted the porters and became spooked. I caught a glimpse of the gorilla as his massive body came tearing into the open, displaying a fierce-looking set of canine teeth. I've been taught never to run from gorillas, but to assume either a submissive fetal position or stand and take the charge, which is usually a bluff. When I saw Beatsme coming, and the porters *going*, and caught a glimpse of Lorna diving into a patch of stinging nettles to the side of the trail, I didn't hesitate for a second to do the same. At the very last moment, almost within arms' reach of me, the animal veered off to the side and disappeared into the forest. Then all grew very quiet. After we gathered our shaken wits, we began the long walk home, my face on fire from contact with the tiny thorns. My clothes were wet again, but this time it wasn't the weather.

We got back to camp at about 2:00 PM and saw Nick soon after, returning from his adventures with Group Five. His face was ashen and his clothes looked like he'd been buried underground for days. It seems that Pablo, the feisty male who threw me on my second day, was provoked by the resident veterinarian or one of the researchers and grabbed for the nearest object, which happened to be Nick. Pablo didn't let go until he had dragged him twenty yards through the undergrowth, tearing Nick's big 300 millimeter lens right out of its camera mount. Nick wasn't hurt, but he's stiff and unnerved. I tried to service the lens with the few tools in my kit, but the lens mount is stripped.

Because tonight was Thursday, we were invited to eat with the guides, two men of the Twa pygmy group; it'll be our turn to reciprocate on Monday. After dinner, we exchanged stories and music. Nick had brought along his little Walkman with a couple of amplified speakers. He played a new cut I've just finished called "Fish Wrap," a composition generated from sampled fish and whale vocalizations. All the percussion is made up of fish; the lead musical lines are samples from Humphrey's voice (see page 51), along with other humpbacks I recorded a few years ago in Hawaii, some killer whales and a walrus. I tried my best to describe what a whale is in French, our only common language. I told the guides it's an animal that breathes air, sometimes grows to 30 meters in length, and lives in the ocean. One of the guides grabbed me by the arm, pulled me outside, and paced off 30 meters (98 feet). He shook his head vigorously, and thrusting a finger in my chest said, "Impossible!" He has no concept of *ocean*, much less whale. He can only visualize a lake a few days' walk from Karisoke, and couldn't make the connection even when we drew a picture of the animal.

Each night when we return to our cabins there's a ritual to perform. Forest rats scamper everywhere—on the short wooden slab that serves as our kitchen countertop, through the straw matting that hangs on the walls and ceiling, but most of all among our clothing and sleeping bags. We're certainly used to them by now, paying almost no attention except when they get near our dinner plates—then we brush them away with a wave of our hand. We have to remember to shake out our sleeping bags, though, because there are usually several burrowed inside. When I first came to camp my bag was filled with wonderful insulation. Three weeks later, it's just a shell—the rats have extracted most of the ticking for their nests. So I sleep almost fully clothed to stay warm during the sometimes-frigid evenings. The rats have also eaten the lining of my favorite winter jacket, which is now just a hollow remnant of what it was. Our food is kept in heavy metal lockers. The items that have to breathe are hung outside in screened containers attached to the shelter structure.

Oddly, however, we've become comfortable in this setting. It is, indeed, a forest paradise that is all too rare.

May 31, 1996

Dian Fosse's research camp was completely destroyed during the terrible recent fighting between the Tutsi and Hutu tribes in Rwanda, though only a few of the rare mountain gorillas weren't accounted for. However, there have been recent reports of gorilla poaching and further destruction in the area. The 70,000-acre Virunga habitat of the mountain gorilla in Rwanda is under constant pressure. Local residents rely on wood fires to warm their earthen huts, and the mountain hillsides within the park—though protected by law—are the only reliable source of wood and bamboo. When the French and Belgian colonials left they took the valuable wood with them. The only natural forest left in the entire country is the gorilla habitat. Nearly everything else is under cultivation.

(CD Track 6)
Green Meadow Stream

June 15, 1989
Lincoln Meadow at Yuba Pass
High Sierras, California

When I arrived at this spot two weeks ago snow covered the meadow where I sit now, recording amid sprouting wildflowers. Trickling water etches delicate traces through the melting banks of snow. Birds nest on the newly exposed grasses all around me. They are so unruffled by my presence that I can walk about without upsetting any of the females and there are nests full of eggs everywhere, settled in tufts of grass and among the low bushes and trees around my campsite.

Streams are among the most difficult natural sounds to record, because on tape they often don't sound anything like they do in the wilderness. I've spent several days capturing the right perspectives to mix into a cohesive composition that will evoke a sense of this peaceful place.

April 30, 1996

Lincoln Meadow at Yuba Pass does not exist anymore. It's gone, all logged out. I went back a couple of years ago with a friend who wanted to see it and it had changed beyond recognition. What's left of the stream is muddied with sediment stirred up by eroded soil from the clear-cutting in the forest above the meadow. A logging company has leveled every tree beyond the casual visitor's line of sight. Originally, they left a 200-yard stand of growth along the road so it would appear that there was a forest, but a short walk into the woods revealed the true story. Now, even that barrier has disappeared; as of this year there's no access to Lincoln Meadow at all. The road is closed and presumably *all* the trees are gone. Of course, there's no longer any vegetation to maintain the integrity of this once-fertile terrain. I look around me and see a muddy stream that once ran clear. I used to stand by the bank and see numerous fish in the deeper pools. The birds and frogs that once sang in great numbers at this time of year are now few in number. Sad to say, but of the 3,300 hours of natural sound I have recorded since 1968, twenty percent of our library comes from now-extinct habitats.

Humphrey: The Rescue

In previous chapters, I described how natural sound has provided a source of material for contemporary musical and ambient compositions. But sound plays a formidable role in contemporary medicine, building construction and architecture, and other branches of science as well. It is so integral to an animal's environment and so important to its sense of well-being that, in some cases, it can even be used to help free trapped creatures, or soothe those in captivity in zoos and theme parks. However, convincing people of the sophisticated ways in which sound may be used can be a problem. The rescue of Humphrey, a humpback whale who became an international celebrity, is a case in point. The following excerpts are from my diary of the period:

Wednesday, October 16, 1985

I got a frantic call from Peigin Barrett, Director of the California Marine Mammal Center in Sausalito, who told me there was a whale in San Francisco Bay. The animal was first sighted six days ago. There's concern, she said, because the bay's saline content isn't high enough for the animal to survive for very long.

Smaller whales like the California gray are often found in the Bay during migration. This is a humpback, and the wayward creature has already become the center of a media circus. It has moved through the open Bay and is heading east, Peigin says, past the Sacramento Delta and into a narrow slough where it appears to be trapped. According to Mammal Center biologists, its breathing is shallow, and its skin shows signs of sloughing. There's concern that brain-swelling *(edema)* from osmotic pressure changes—resulting from the low salt content so far from the whale's ocean habitat—could kill it.

I told Peigin that although I worked with humpbacks while doing research on my Ph.D., I know only a little about them, like most researchers. I have experience with marine bio-acoustics, having recorded humpback mating songs in Hawaii, but don't know anything about their vocal behavior outside that environment. As far as I know, no one is sure what sounds a humpback might respond to— whether they might frighten or attract it. Nothing has ever been published on the matter.

A local researcher played some killer whale sounds to try to scare the animal back to the ocean, but without success. He stopped because the animal seemed to be under too much stress. Peigin asked me to pull together equipment and technicians to try our own sound experiments. But she warned that her group has no funds for the operation, and expects little cooperation from the National Marine Fisheries Service (NMFS), who seem to want to direct the operation from 400 miles away in Long Beach. (NMFS enforces the Marine Mammal Protection Act, and governs what people can and can't do about marine mammal rescue operations under the constraints of federal law. Normally, one can't get within 100 yards of a protected marine mammal without a special permit, and under very few circumstances can an animal be harassed. The penalties for noncompliance are severe.) Several environmental groups are fighting for leadership of the operation, according to Peigin, in spite of NMFS's claim to authority. None of them can decide which rescue agency to support, or whether they themselves should lead the operation.

My gut tells me this one could get crazy. No money, lots of aggravation. I took a deep breath and told Peigin I would help.

I called some acquaintances who work for the Navy. Generously, they offered to loan me a $17,000 underwater Navy loudspeaker, and to deliver it to my house in San Francisco this evening—though it means a 240-mile round trip from Monterey. No sooner was I off the phone when Peigin called again, saying we needed to cancel the underwater speaker. Sheridan Stone from NMFS in Long Beach had just called her to say he was coming to San Francisco with his boss, Jim Leckey (West Coast Director of NMFS) to make an on-site assessment tomorrow. It's NMFS's contention that because the whale has been in the delta for just a week they want to see if it can survive on its own. I believe the animal will die if we don't try something. And I couldn't reach my Navy buddies; they were already on the road.

After sending the equipment back to Monterey, totally

embarrassed, I called a colleague, Dr. Dianna Reiss. Turns out she and Peigin are friends. She suggested we drive to Rio Vista—a small town on the Sacramento River where the whale has been spotted—tomorrow to get a clearer picture for ourselves.

Thursday, October 17

The Mammal Center helps stranded marine mammals to recover from illnesses, including the all too common problem of gunshot wounds, then rehabilitates and releases them back to their environments. Guided by a volunteer staff, it's become a thriving, helpful organization, providing aid to thousands of stranded creatures.

All day they've been flooded by calls from "experts" and the press. One of the volunteers showed me a list of suggestions for saving the animal that have come in. These include dropping ice into the water so the whale will be more comfortable, dropping a curtain behind him so he can't go backward, and dangling a piece of raw meat in front of him to lure him away! There's lots of scurrying around, but no one knows what to do. Someone from a local paper suggested calling the whale Humphrey, and it seems to have stuck. He's being propelled from anonymity to media stardom. If only trapped human beings got so much attention.

I phoned Dr. Ken Norris at U. C. Santa Cruz. He's the director of Environmental Studies there, and knows as much as anyone about whales. He suggested that we try the *Oikomi* pipes, but says the NMFS folks won't listen to him. The pipes are eight-foot metal tubes, one end of which is submerged in the water. When the other end is hit with a hammer by folks in a boat, the jarring noise sometimes drives marine mammals away—the method was developed by

Japanese fishermen to herd dolphins close to shore so they could be slaughtered for dog food. Ken asked me to reinforce his suggestion with NMFS, and to keep him posted.

There's only one pay phone at the station for the press and everyone else; and it has been an instrument of high tension, since everyone wants to use it. We're having an Indian summer, so I stretched out on the grass in the late afternoon sun. Peigin came by to tell me that a boat had been found to take us to see Humphrey.

The *Sportfish*, approximately 26 feet long and set up for striped bass, is Jack Findleton's boat. He's a short, stocky Vietnam vet, and head of the California Striped Bass Association. He speaks with a machine-gun voice, as if he's shouting orders to a platoon; his intensity makes me feel withdrawn around him. Besides Dianna and Peigin, a couple of researchers—Mark and Debbie Ferrari—and a Time-Life photographer accompanied us. Using some of Dianna's equipment, I took readings of the river by recording with a hydrophone (an underwater microphone) a hundred yards north and south of the Rio Vista bridge.

We hoped to discover what's attracting Humphrey's attention, luring him from the salt water environments he's used to. The noise of traffic driving over the bridge gets transmitted through the pilings into the water, I quickly discovered, and *cavitation* (signature noise) from boat propellers makes the waterway pretty noisy. Maybe the animal is being drawn to the bridges—I want to explore this idea when I get back to the lab.

We headed up to Cache and Prospect Sloughs and there was the animal, swimming around, exhibiting what appeared to be feeding behavior, though—since no humpback has been observed in these waters before—no one knew for sure. Humphrey was leaving "footprints," pool-like formations on the surface of the water, a result of the motion of his flukes, as he swam in elliptical paths. The Ferraris observed that he seemed to be breathing normally, though his skin is definitely turning gray, and showing sings of blistering. They didn't know whether this was a result of an earlier beaching in Oakland, the effects of sunburn, or—worse—edema. We're beginning to realize how little we know, and it's frustrating.

We wanted to find out if the whale was interested in food—a sign of good health if he is. Because schools of fish appeared on Findleton's fish scope, a couple of researchers suspected he's been drawn to an available food source.

Humphrey continued to swim near where the fish appeared, but I felt doubtful. The number of fish on the scope didn't seem to get smaller, so I suspect he hasn't grown too hungry yet. The water was 40 feet deep at that point, and we decided to do more sound tests. Nothing. Just the sounds of a hydrophone beginning to malfunction. Lots of pops and hissing. I changed the connector from the hydrophone cable to my recorder and things quieted down.

It was getting late, so we returned to San Francisco for an evening meeting. A group of talented biologists has formed around the issue, and I feel encouraged by their enthusiasm.

At the meeting, NMFS made it clear that the group from the Marine Mammal Center was operating "outside" the authorized team of government scientists; we were cautioned to be careful. Because they have no one available to address cold water sciences—the arcane scientific realm under which humpbacks fall—their best recommendations were limited to quick fixes like cracker shells and seal bombs (underwater explosives which detonate on contact with the water, used to frighten marine mammals or fish that exhibit behavior NMFS deems improper) or to do nothing. It's their opinion nothing can be done anyway. A rescue would be expensive, and no one has a budget to pay for it.

I proposed to our group that we find a moderating influence, someone with enough personal and political presence to guide NMFS to more moderate positions. They agreed it was a good idea, but when I called congressmen, senators and marine consultants over a period of many hours and received no help, it was clear that the issue was either too hot or just low priority. We called the local CBS station again, and a woman in the newsroom who'd grown tired of hearing from us provided state Senator John Garamendi's home number, warning us not to reveal who we got it from.

As luck would have it Garamendi was home, and delighted we'd called. "I came home for dinner and told my wife I felt frustrated. I wanted to help with the rescue, but didn't know where to turn." Dianna and I gave him the scenario, and he asked for time to consider options. He called back almost immediately to say he'll be at the Coast Guard Station tomorrow morning with as many federal, state and local representatives as he can summon. Helicopters, barges, tugs, small boats and other support personnel will accompany him. He'll enlist whatever other agencies we need to help. We were all dead tired, but his confidence energized us.

Friday, October 18, 11:00AM
Rio Vista Coast Guard Station

For the first time in my life I was impressed with a politician. Anybody who can muster as much help as Garamendi promised in such a short time must have his act together. Wanting to be adequately prepared, I stayed up most of the night reviewing the literature on cold water science and whales.

Everyone gathered at the Coast Guard Station. Garamendi had managed to pull favors from a local contractor who prepared pipes for us to bang, though no one will get to use them for a while. There was no organization. No one had figured how many pipes and boats we'll need after the animal leaves the 50-yard narrows of Cache or Prospect Slough and swims out into bodies of water miles across. One thing became clear, though: everyone wants to get the animal out. Everyone except the NMFS people, that is.

Garamendi's first move was to eliminate the press from our discussions. This had the tempering effect of focusing energy on the task at hand, instead of theatrics. Still, there were many views and interests.

It quickly became apparent NMFS wanted control. Stone and Leckey had discussed the matter with their bosses at the National Oceanic and Atmospheric Administration, and the agency wanted to avoid making a decision for a while longer. They invoked their authority to restrain our enthusiasm, expressing various concerns about costs. During a break I even heard one of them in the hall, suggesting that when the animal died—which should be soon he guessed—they'd hire the California Conservation Corps to cut him up and bury his parts.

Findleton was optimistic, though, his attitude infectious. So was Garamendi's. But that didn't change the situation: after Dianna and I presented a summary of known science, it was obvious no one had enough information to make decisions. We know that to mount a successful rescue we'll be applying new techniques, probably generating new science in the area of acoustics and its effect on whales. Garamendi emerged from the meeting as operation director. The NMFS folks sat across the room with scowls on their faces, arms folded tightly. They'd lost control and didn't know what to do.

Garamendi asked who wanted to be in charge of the scientific component. Everyone looked in my direction; since

Dianna and I had just given our summary, it appeared as if we knew something. I in turn looked at Dianna, who averted her gaze. As no one else would do it, I was designated Scientific Director, though I made Dianna promise that she'll be with me at all times. She knows more about current whale science than I do.

The meeting resumed, and we made the case for Ken Norris' Oikomi idea. The pipe solution is modest, and will offer the animal a chance without destroying its hearing. Stone and Leckey still preferred seal bombs, which we believe might seriously harm the animal. They want fast results, but otherwise expressed the conviction it's a no-win cause. Even though there's great optimism among the group, we all wondered deep down if they weren't right.

As I looked around the room, it struck me that most of the members of our odd assembly would never otherwise be able to agree about where to eat lunch, let alone decide how to free a whale.

The NMFS folks checked with their absentee boss, Charlie Fullerton, and decided to let the whale ride out the weekend without interference; they won't be pushed into action. In the meantime, they told us to start preparing for the pipe operation, in case the animal shows serious deterioration. Mark and Debbie Ferrari were chosen to monitor the animal's health, and Findleton to direct the flotilla of volunteers and boats he's assembling. Dianna and I, meanwhile, are pulling together a group of advisors familiar with humpback whale science, in an effort to establish alternative plans.

Saturday-Sunday, October 19-20

Dutra Construction, the firm that supplied us with the pipes, generously made their helicopter available to me all weekend; I visited Humphrey both days with their help.

I've been recording the whale at every opportunity. Sunday morning we got a report that he couldn't be located. Apparently, he slipped by all of the observers and the Coast Guard boats during the night. A bit later, we got word he had ended up in Shag Slough, a shallow fresh water channel a couple of hundred yards long and 80 feet wide located between two heavily fertilized fields. He was found swimming back and forth between an old wooden bridge at one end and the high dirt banks along the sides. A group from UC Berkeley tested the water and determined that toxins were leaching into the slough from surrounding fields, with high levels of selenium and PCBs both present. We have no idea how these might affect the whale.

Humphrey had somehow managed to swim past the rotten pilings below the water at high tide with little problem. A few boaters were given permission to try to herd him with the noise of their engines. But he seemed unwilling or unable to swim under the bridge in the opposite direction. Meanwhile, a couple of tattooed punks on the opposite bank began pelting Humphrey with beer cans each time he surfaced. I called the police on my cell phone. After several minutes, the highway patrol appeared and led them away. I'm worried for the animal and for the people trying to help him.

We continued to record Humphrey for several hours, but there was a lot of boat noise from curious powerboaters, though the Coast Guard had sealed the entrance to the channel where Humphrey was trapped. We got occasional click sounds we thought were coming from the whale, which we'll analyze later. Some of them suggested a type of *echolocation* (a sonar-like sound produced by some whales to "visualize" objects in their environment). If that is indeed what they are, it would be the first time humpback echolocation has been recorded.

Monday, October 21

I'm unable to determine conclusively whether Humphrey's using echolocation; we've picked up sounds we can't identify. The clicks we heard yesterday may also be the downshifting of gears from boats in or near the slough. I spent hours analyzing the recordings but can't be sure. In the meantime, NMFS continues to refuse our appeals for action.

Tuesday, October 22

Early in the morning I drove to Shag Slough, to record the whale again and evaluate its condition, and to speak with Garamendi about a meeting planned for tomorrow. Mark and Debbie Ferrari are getting good data with help from California Conservation Corps volunteers monitoring the animal. They're reassured by the positive reports.

Because of the intense media coverage, pressure has mounted on NMFS to become more pro-active. We've convinced them to try driving the animal out of the slough with the pipes, as far into the main channel as we can, and hopefully down river. We decided to be diplomatic and make it seem like it's NMFS's idea.

Wednesday, October 23

During the last few days we've been in contact with eight scientists about the rescue—Ken Norris, Joe Geraci, Bill Watkins, Peter Tyack, Barent Wursig, Robert Hoffman, John Twiss and Laurie Gage, a veterinarian. We've reviewed the literature, but are unable to shed any light on the problem. This morning we again considered options. They include seal bombs, strobe lights and a crane-suspended sling, whose offerer expects the 40-ton untrained Humphrey to leap into it so we can hoist him onto a barge and carry him to open water. The pipe plan won a vote of confidence from all eight consultants and our group; if the pipes work the Conservation Corps will drop a weighted curtain over the side of the bridge after the whale passes so it can't return to the slough.

It's Findleton's job to lead the boaters in orchestrated fashion, and Dutra's responsibility to bring along about two dozen of the pipes and hammers to bang them. Peigin assumed responsibility for assembling 100 volunteers through her resources at the Mammal Center. At last, everyone's focused on a rescue. The energy we get from working together helps overcome the fatigue we're beginning to feel.

Thursday, October 24

We gathered at the Rio Vista marina just after sunrise; it was another bright-hazy Indian Summer day. Findleton seemed uptight. Turned out he wanted one of his buddies—who'd been assigned to another boat—to travel with us. There wasn't room; the positions were pre-assigned, and we were too short on pipes to create another crew. He remained intense and quiet, except for his proclivity to bark orders, eyes fixed straight ahead on the beautiful autumn morning, refusing to be engaged in conversation.

Each of the eight small boats carried three or four volunteers—one to hammer, one to secure the pipes to the gunwales, and a driver to keep the integrity of the crescent-shaped flotilla intact. The boats were equipped with radios so Findleton could direct. Dianna remained at Liberty Island Bridge with my Nagra, recording the sounds of the pipes and—we hoped—responses from the whale.

The Coast Guard issued a directive to boaters to stay away from the site or anywhere that Humphrey might be headed. At 10:30AM we began maneuvering the boats into position at Shag Slough's north end. We could see Dianna with her recorder at the bridge. The whale was soon sighted by Mark Ferrari halfway down the slough. The order was given to put the boats into gear, just a bit faster than idle speed, and to strike the pipes.

Until then, Humphrey had seemed lethargic. But as soon as the pipe noise was transmitted into the water, a different whale revealed himself—immediately, he responded. As the boats advanced, Humphrey moved south, keeping well ahead of the flotilla that was now spread across the 80-foot width of the slough. When he got to the bridge, though, the whale stopped dead in his wake, rolled onto his side, exposed one large fin and would not go under. The boat crews made several passes at him, but he wouldn't budge.

It turns out that earlier in the week at the bridge site, Findleton discovered what looked like rotted pilings on his fish scope, just below the surface of the water at the widest gap between the visible pilings and the deepest water. Though this is the broadest space between the new pilings, apparently the whale is aware of the old pilings, and believes them to be obstacles. He appeared reluctant to swim over them again, as he must have done when he entered several days before. Perhaps he injured himself the first time through. Debbie Ferrari ordered Findleton to stop the operation so the whale would not get stressed. At first he seemed put off by her order, but then he told the other boats to cool it.

We tried again later, but the animal eluded us, swimming past or underneath the boats, in opposite directions or stopping just short of the bridge. Back at the Coast Guard station I met with Garamendi, Findleton and Bill Dutra. Any rescue now appears to be a matter of removing the bridge, or at least the old pilings. Dutra offered to blow up the bridge, since it's destined for removal anyway. Garamendi asked Dutra if he could just remove the old pilings. Dutra didn't know, but said he'd try to figure something out.

Friday, October 25

I talked to Dutra, who told me that his crew did a little work early this morning, removing some obstacles at the bridge's widest gap, but none of the submerged pilings. They couldn't hook the rotting timbers in an effective way, and didn't want to use explosives so close to Humphrey.

For most of the day nothing happened, but at about 4:15 PM I got a call from Garamendi's press secretary, telling me the whale had moved past the bridge. "Findleton and his crew have done it!" he shouted into the phone. I was delighted; at the same time, I realized that while we've moved the animal 200 yards, there are 65 miles to go to open sea. That'll take a lot of pipes and boats, particularly when Humphrey gets into stretches of open delta water several miles across.

Late tonight I got a call from a friend at one of the TV stations, telling me the animal has moved seven miles downstream. He's been sighted very close to Rio Vista.

Saturday, October 26

To my distraction, I've been subpoenaed to appear as a forensic witness in a drug case, in the Virgin Islands! When I checked into my hotel in St. Thomas after the tedious flight, there were a dozen messages from Rio Vista and the press. I've never felt so far away from home! I called Garamendi's office first, and learned that the whale has moved as far as the Rio Vista bridge, but has refused to go under the structure. In apparent frustration—and without consulting any of the biologists or Garamendi—Sheridan

Stone sneaked a shotgun aboard Findleton's boat and fired a seal bomb into the water behind where the whale was swimming, in front of nearly 10,000 people gathered on the river bank! Shortly after that, Humphrey beached himself.

I called the Mammal Center for confirmation—they were hysterical. If I'd been there I'd have had Stone arrested, under the terms of the same Marine Protection Act that he used to prevent our rescue attempts.

I spent the evening at the Virgin Island law library, reviewing the Act. I concluded that what Stone did is illegal, punishable by heavy fines and possibly jail. I wanted to see him arrested and start proceedings.

When I called Garamendi back I read him the part of the Act that applied to harassment; I told him what I wanted done. The Senator sounded tired. He spent forty-five minutes explaining that he understood my reaction. He told me he felt the same way, but thought it important to consider the outcome if we proceeded. He was persuasive; I relented. If the animal has a chance, I realize, we need all the help we can get. The Senator told me Stone was remorseful and, in fact, said he'd have Stone call me.

Stone called a while later and we talked. We're trying to solve the same problem, but with different agendas.

Tuesday, October 29

Back in San Francisco. The whale has been moving up and down the Sacramento River, staying near bridges with enough automobile traffic to transmit noise to the water below; the auto and truck noise must be attracting the animal. Findleton and his stalwarts shepherd Humphrey five to ten miles downstream each day, only to find that he has returned back upriver the next morning, toward the Rio Vista bridge. They have no way to prevent him from doing so.

By now we're all mystified, and the NMFS folks have scaled back the operation. I called Garamendi's office and learned one last effort will be mounted. We're to meet at the California Water Resources Board in Sacramento for an international teleconference of scientists and concerned parties.

Thursday, October 31
Sacramento

The conference began at a little after 10:00am, in an atmosphere of guarded optimism. Many of those who have been working since the operation began, however, are exhausted.

At half past twelve we began to consider options. Lou Herman, a biologist from the University of Hawaii, suggested it might be worth trying to lure the whale *to* some sound instead of trying to repel it. He told us his group tried some playback experiments in Hawaii, and that certain humpback feeding sounds drew the animals to underwater speakers where vocalizations were playing. If we used a suitable system like a Navy J-11 underwater speaker, he said, and locate it downstream from the animal, luring might be successful.

"Perhaps we can get a tape recording of your sounds from you," Dianna told him. "But what will keep the animal from getting habituated to the playback, especially if there are no fish around to feed them?"

Herman chuckled, and told us he was surprised that the experiment worked so well; humpback whales weren't known to feed in Hawaiian waters. Still, the animals were more attracted to the feeding sounds than to any humpback or synthetic sound they tried. He suggested we use his sounds for short periods of time until the animal is attracted, then turn them off, beginning again when the animal gets off track. We accepted his offer, and—just in case—obtained as backup another source of humpback feeding sounds from Duane Johnson of California Fish and Game.

I checked with Findleton to see if he had 120 volts on his boat, which we'll need to power our amplifiers and tape playback machines. He doesn't, but said he'll help us find a boat that does. When I called Herman later, I asked for detailed information about the experiments.

Friday-Saturday, November 1-2

Herman's package arrived; it contained a two-paragraph description and an audio cassette. The letter says that the tape is a twenty-minute loop, originally played back on a Sony cassette recorder attached to an 800-watt amplifier that powered the J-11 underwater speaker. It says humpback whales were lured from as far as two kilometers away. I know quite well the J-11 can't handle 800 watts, since it's rated at a maximum of 200 and will be destroyed if you give it that much power. Since sound travels quickly in water; two kilometers isn't impressive. As for the decibel rating, I don't trust Herman's data—there's no information included about how he set up his instrumentation. His students gathered their data from studies with free-ranging animals in normal salt water, not a trapped animal in a fresh water river and slough, suffering everything from disorientation to edema. Finally, I realized, he provided no information about the duration of the tests performed.

When I put the cassette on my machine its quality was dreadful, confirming my worst fears. Field recordings made for experiments are typically poor, but these are terrible. There are lots of extraneous noises on the cassette and it's just one segment, fifty-five seconds in length repeated over and over. This may have worked under relaxed conditions in Hawaii, but our situation is more problematical. If the idea is to work at all, especially given Diana's worries about the whale growing habituated to it, the recording will need to be cleaned up and altered. I have a vision of no sleep for the next three days.

I called Dianna and asked if she could find out who did the original recordings; I wanted to speak directly with those involved. We haven't been provided enough information by Herman, in the teleconference or in his letter. At my expense, I rented a local recording studio with a digital Kurtzweil sampling synthesizer and lots of digital and analog processing gear, and went to work. With a device originally developed for the FBI and the Federal Avation Administration, I removed the unwanted noise on the recording. Mostly it consisted of boat engines, because the recordist forgot or was unable to get the engine stopped when the tape was made. Despite the fact that the original was only 55 seconds long, the process took six hours to accomplish. Though I was feeling overwhelmed by the task, one thing is certain—what I learn will add useful information to literature on such work.

Then came the hard part. I knew that we would have to have at least a fifteen-to-twenty minute tape of different-sounding segments so that it would appear natural to the animal. I know from my work in Hawaii that humpback vocalizations, though often similar, are almost never repeated the same way twice.

The boat engine noise was reduced without destroying the integrity of the feeding sounds, and the cleaned up short segment programmed into a sampler. I changed the duration, pitch, reverberation, amplitude (loudness) over time, even the timbre (texture) of the material, recombining and mixing the various blends so it wouldn't sound repetitive. I've worked on outrageous rock and roll sessions that were easier and faster!

The session began at mid-afternoon on Friday and continued through the night, all day Saturday and late into the evening. During a break, I called Dianna to ask if she had learned more about the experiments. She told me that she'd spoken with Joe Mobley, the student who performed the Hawaiian studies. He told her that when the experiment was proposed, Herman balked at the idea. Mobley continued despite Herman's opposition, which explained why Herman was surprised by the results!

Mobley told Dianna that Scott Baker, another student in Herman's program, recorded the feeding sounds in Alaska during 1984. I asked her if she realized that none of Herman's comments at the teleconference or in the letter mentioned his students or what they contributed. She responded that this was standard operating procedure among some researchers.

Sunday, November 3

The Bootlegger, the boat Findleton arranged for us, picked us up at 8:00AM at the marina opposite Brown's Island in Pittsburgh. Dianna, her husband Stuart Finklestein, Larry Burr, a photographer, a woman I'm dating and myself were assigned to the command boat. Greg Pless and Brian Wilson joined us from the Navy Post-Graduate School in Monterey, bearing the precious J-11 underwater speaker and amplifier—considering how we treated them at the beginning of the operation, when I sent them back to Monterey with no warning, I'm surprised by their continued generosity. I brought the Nagra and several copies of the tape I'd labored over, in case one copy failed or broke during playback.

The boat, a 40-foot cabin cruiser, picked us up at 10:00 AM, and we began to move upriver toward Antioch where the whale was last sighted. By sheer determination and endurance, Findleton and his volunteer boaters had managed to move Humphrey fourteen miles—more like a hundred and fifty if one took into account the retreats and advances they've endured these past ten days. That's a lot of pipe-banging, and Findleton is one of the heroes of the operation.

As we approached Antioch we couldn't actually see the animal, but heard on the marine radio that it had been sighted in the San Joaquin Delta upriver from where we were. Near the Antioch Bridge in the diffuse autumn morning light, the river seemed filled with boats—hundreds of them, stretched over a mile across from shore to shore. Helicopters from all the national TV networks dotted the skies, generating an incredible amount of noise—they wouldn't stay at the distances the FAA had set for the operation, at least one half mile horizontally and 1,000 feet off ground.

We couldn't be bothered about that now, though. Over the radio came a directive from the NMFS's Charlie Fullerton: we had five minutes from 11:00 AM to try our sounds. If they worked, fine—if not, we were to get off the water so the pipe drive could start.

Under pressure, we set up our equipment. We lowered the 120-pound speaker into the water off the bow to a depth of ten feet. A solid mass of stainless steel, it looked like a squat cylinder with rubber diaphragms attached to both ends. We could put a maximum of 200 watts through the speaker but wanted to be conservative, so we set our levels at a maximum of 168 watts. We were ready.

Looking off the stern of our boat pointed to the east, I was reminded of the Normandy invasion. There were private volunteer vessels, Navy vessels, boats from the Coast Guard, Marines, Army and National Guard—perhaps 200 boats in all. It was the first time I had ever heard of these suckers working together in war or peace. In the middle of the whole fleet and at the very front stood the press boat, so full of people, cameras, and other gear it bristled like a porcupine in the thermals rising off the river. It listed badly to starboard, but the Coast Guard—so careful about overloaded vessels ordinarily—must have been looking the other way.

Fullerton barked at us to start the tape; suddenly, he was boss. We were now a quarter mile away from the animal. I switched on the recorder with the reconfigured tape and, at first—because I was in the cabin—was unaware of what had happened. It didn't take long to find out. The whale made a run for our boat, covering the 400 yards between us in fifteen seconds. He came so fast that when he finally arrived, his nose nudged the underwater speaker at our bow. His body, which by now was alongside the *Bootlegger*—two feet longer than the entire 40-foot vessel—caused the boat to list so badly the port deck was nearly awash. We were terrified we might capsize, overwhelmed by the whale's behavior. Jim Cook and his wife Sandy, the boat's owners, looked like they'd seen a ghost.

I recovered my composure and shouted at Jim to put the boat in gear, but dead slow. He did, and to our wonder, Humphrey tucked his head to our stern, just as if he'd discovered a long-lost friend. Perhaps he recognized the voice we were transmitting. I told Jim to move the boat a bit faster, up to nearly six knots, and to hold that speed. He did and the whale continued to follow us.

Using the protocol Joe Mobley described to Dianna, we used the sounds sparingly. The machine was turned on when the animal seemed distracted, or when he veered in another direction. I stopped the tape when he followed in our wake—we had over forty miles to go, and I didn't want the animal to get used to my best record production to date. Finally, I had produced an irresistible hit!

The Coast Guard cutter *Point Hyer* cleared a mile-wide path for us on the river, ordering all other vessels out of the way. For the next several hours the cutter was the only boat we saw, more than half a mile ahead. We were alone on the river with Humphrey and he never stopped moving.

The press helicopters, however, were still an annoyance. We felt they were distracting the whale, coming in lower and lower with each pass until, in one case, we saw water roiling in the blades' downwash as one tried to get a close-up. It's then that I began to use the hand-held radio. I got the FAA on the horn and told them to get the choppers out of the area with all other aircraft. I asked Travis Air Force Base's Air Traffic Control tower to divert all flight approaches, takeoffs and landings to the north of the field, and to clear the area in the hope we could stretch our luck.

We were 10 miles downstream when the operation was interrupted. Fullerton got on the radio and ordered us to stop the playback, to cut our engines so that he could tag the animal. NMFS had tried to shoot tags into the whale when it was still near the Rio Vista bridge; the tags pierced Humphrey's sensitive skin, but he sloughed them off. Now Fullerton wanted to use a more powerful projectile.

Dianna and I had no patience for such nonsense. She warned Fullerton she was finished with the rescue if he persisted. She told him that there were several ways to identify whales developed by researchers Peter Tyack and Ken Balcomb, that he could use them if he cared to. Humphrey, she pointed out, was now history's most photographed whale. We had fluke silhouette photos to identify him no matter where he shows up; there was no need to jeopardize the momentum of the rescue.

Fullerton was adamant. So were we. Since we had the

more powerful hand-held transmitter, I simply held down the "send-receive" button so no one could transmit or receive and ordered Jim Cook to keep going. Thankfully, he complied, and that was the end of the discussion.

Or so we thought. When I finally released the button half an hour later an enraged Fullerton came on the air, and warned us that he would arrest us if we pulled such a stunt again. Of course, we weren't too alarmed, because the issue—as far as we were concerned—was resolved, and the press was monitoring and recording everything. We had the recording, and the whale, after all, was moving.

Humphrey, meanwhile, had captivated us all, leaving our wake to swim close to the shoreline of every river town we passed. At Martinez, Port Costa and Crockett, where townspeople lined the shore, he swam over to the river banks and either did a full breach or a tail slap, sending plumes of water into the air to the crowds' delight. It was as if he was thanking them for their support. We heard cheers and gleeful shouts a mile out on the river after each display.

The other miracle was that this creature—which everyone thought was ill, incapacitated or crazy—followed our recording for seven hours, covering nearly fifty miles from Antioch to just off Angel Island in San Francisco Bay before we lost him in the darkness Sunday night.

Monday, November 4

I'm at home with a bad case of the flu. I hear reports on the marine radio that the whale was located this morning off Point Richmond near the Brothers Islands. Typical of November weather, the region has been covered with prewinter overcast; Humphrey was difficult to spot (according to Dianna and several others who have called), and swam around the bay, appearing to avoid contact with the rescue team. The Findleton-Bootlegger team tried the pipes and our feeding sounds to lure him, pursuing him all day until finally, just before nightfall, he turned west and swam out beneath the Golden Gate.

Postscript

A year after Humphrey was rescued, we still weren't certain what led him into the Bay—we can only speculate. Early in October '85 the weather was extremely calm, and there was no wave action along the shore of Northern California. Perhaps some migrating whales use waves along the shore as an audio reference for their travels. While shore wave action was virtually non-existent in early October, noise transmitted through the pilings of the Golden Gate Bridge (and other bridges along Humphrey's path) by the auto traffic may have been similar enough to draw the animal off course. A comparison of the recordings we made at various bridges the whale passed under and offshore wave action when it resumed revealed very similar patterns. It's only a guess; we may never know.

One day, some time ago, I dreamt of creating an audio journey that would guide the listener from the seashore to the depths of the ocean and back again. It would be a way to convey the drama of the environment and what Humphrey and his ocean associates listen to daily. (Part of that idea is heard in "A Gift from the Sea.") Little by little, we're beginning to understand that most of these creatures produce some kind of sound. We're just now beginning to look at their communication. Much mystery remains. Some of my older colleagues have remarked that we're having so much fun trying to discover the answers, we hope the revelation never comes.

A Higher Kinship

The short samples and experiences included here represent just a fraction of my work in the medium of natural sound. But such sound has become very difficult to obtain. When I began this process in 1968, it took roughly 200 hours to get an hour of material good enough to use on a recording. It now takes nearly 2,000 hours to get the same amount of material. Disappearing habitats and human noise are encroaching on the natural world with incredible rapidity.

On a recent trip to Costa Rica's Osa Peninsula the destruction was more than we had expected. With my colleague, Doug Quin, I recorded nearly eighteen hours a day on average. Since it was the beginning of the wet season, it rained for some part of every day, was very hot (over 95 degrees) and quite humid (80 - 85%+). Mostly, rain came in the afternoon and after midnight, leaving some rain-free periods.

While we were able to record between storm cells, we couldn't avoid the devastating effects of the logging and farming that have occurred since I was last there, just seven years ago. Wide logging roads have been cut through the forest, creating routes that intersect with other roads or farms. These carve out what scientists call "biological islands" (parks are sometimes more benign examples of such habitats). The roads are so wide and impassable that the creatures who live in the canopy, which includes most tropical rain forest wildlife, are confined to relatively small tracts of a few hundred to a thousand acres. Except for birds and some flying insects, many animals can't cross into their otherwise normal turf—the forest canopy doesn't reach across the roads.

Howler monkeys are an unfortunate case in point. In lifetimes of several decades, many never set foot on the forest floor. During my prior visit they seemed to be everywhere—we couldn't escape them, visually *or* vocally. This time we never caught a glimpse of one, and only heard three distant single calls in 240 hours on site. Also, the insect-to-bird sound ratio is radically altered; there is far less aural density. The cicadas, meanwhile, have grown louder. This time we heard none of the dawn choruses evident during my last visit, of the sort one expects at this time of year. And no dusk chorus whatsoever.

Something seemed out of balance from the moment we arrived. It was. Though we were lucky to obtain short periods of quiet, there was lots of new noise—the sound of domestic animals from farms that have sprung up nearby, motorcycles straight-piping over the dirt roads and vehicles without mufflers. Because the terrain was hilly and wet these noises carried farther, penetrating deep into what few forest islands were left.

The roads that have been cut through the forest are muddy, insect-ridden swamps, so soupy that our four-wheel drive Land Rover required a serious set of chains to navigate. Often, that wasn't enough. The biological research station we stayed at in Corcovado is experimenting with forest plants that may grow back, with secondary growth. In some cases, vegetation does recover—a little. When we tried to record in secondary growth areas planted twenty to thirty years ago, the mix of clearly defined acoustic voices of insects, birds and mammals was not yet discernible. So although forests sometimes *look* okay, the

story can't be told with the eye alone. Sound analysis helps quantify our impressions. Even without the research, however, I'm afraid we know what has become of this once-bountiful site.

When I return home from months in the forest, I sometimes feel estranged by such insights, cut off from friends and intimates because they haven't shared what I experienced. In the briefest geological span, we've become disengaged from our environment, and evolved to a state of hearing impairment and tone-deafness. It's made us spiritually and psychically impoverished.

Along with our forests and other habitats, we have lost the ability to hear the rhythms of the wilderness. Buried under concrete and steel or burned to the ground, many of them have been lost to us forever. To replace voices we will never hear we have turned, instead, to the study of single animal sounds in an effort to learn more. While we obtain some results from these efforts, we end up deceived. We know the frequency, duration, timbre and prosody of a particular voice, but next to nothing about what is meant by it, or how it evolved. We understand something about the tree, but haven't a clue about the substance or value of the forest. "Must have been a moment when we could have said no," a character in Tom Stoppard's *Rosenkrantz & Gildenstern Are Dead* remarks toward the end of the play. "Somehow we missed it. Oh well, maybe we'll do better next time."

June 21, 1996
Alone at a campsite near Yuba Pass
in California's High Sierras

As I gaze beyond the light of the fire, I sense a time long before we summoned our received gods to show us the way. I was raised in a culture that feared the uncontrolled, yet felt certain of its capacity to control it. My parents, terrified of the natural world and the dangers in it, were even apprehensive about letting me play in the field by our house. But at the same time they instilled a healthy skepticism in me, and the curiosity to seek out other truths; these eventually brought me closer to the land and its diverse creature life.

It has taken me still longer to begin to perceive answers to larger questions that baffled me—to see beyond the deceptive security offered by organized religion, and by our formidable institutions. Only at this late stage in my life (in my late 50s) am I beginning to hear the messages—*musical* messages—that the remarkable organisms so feared by my culture have for eons been sending.

In the end—before the forest echoes die—we may want to listen carefully to this world, to discover that we aren't separate, but a vital part of one fragile biological place. How many of us will hear the message in time? The whisper of every leaf and creature implores us to love the natural sources of our lives, which—indeed—may hold secrets of love for all things, especially our own humanity. This divine music is fast growing dim; the time approaches when we may have to bear witness, as Elizabeth Wilson suggested, when the creature spirits return for one final hunt.

Wild Sanctuary
Glen Ellen, California

Notes From the Studio

"I don't want real, I want magic!"
—Blanche DuBois, in Tennessee Williams's
A Streetcar Named Desire

When the late avant-garde composer John Cage was asked what he thought about natural sound recordings, he dismissed them, saying they were little more than unmediated objects, unworthy of serious consideration despite their obvious relation to his own "found" compositions. Cage was of course referring to sound transferred unedited and unstructured from field to tape, and his experience with some natural sound recordists justified the comment. But Cage missed the point, in part because as an urban composer he was unfamiliar with the field.

In 1968, in collaboration with Paul Beaver, I wrote and produced the first album combining natural sound with traditional composition. Because recording technologies were still deficient then, we were unable to record natural sound with any dynamic that translated adequately to vinyl disk or cassette.

But portable stereo recorders, capable of meeting professional studio standards, soon became available. New microphone systems, able to withstand turbulent and very humid weather, allowed us to record outdoors in ways not previously possible. With the advent of the synthesizer, the definition of music began to change. Worldwide sound art has come to mean—broadly—control or manipulation of sound. This concept was first expressed in the *Nonesuch Guide to Electronic Music*.

Exactly the same model—the notion of control of sound as art—is used in the creation of natural sound compositions. In my work, such sounds are first recorded in remote wilderness locations; the raw material is then edited into smaller related components and transferred to computer or multi-track analog formats.

There are three compositional modes I usually employ with the material. The first is *time*. Frequently, I try to give an idea of the sounds of a habitat from dawn to dusk. The second choice is *space*, as in a journey from one place to another (i. e. the journey of a drop of water from the mountains to the ocean). The two approaches may also be combined. Other approaches include more traditional classical musical forms, such as *sonata allegro* or *rondo*, or popular forms in which particularly beautiful sounds are repeated. Once the material is digitized, many of the animal voices are separated out and recombined into the ambient mix, in much the same way a traditional composer combines voices for an orchestra. At the same time careful attention is paid to the integrity of what is being represented.

By the time I'm ready to compose, I have as many as 200 separate components that will serve as the basis for the composition. Then I carefully map out what sound goes where. *Amazon Days, Amazon Nights*—selections from which appear on the enclosed disc—offers one example. For this album, I began the process of building stereo tracks one by one, each segment taken from a month of environmental recordings gathered from a single field trip. After reviewing nearly 200 hours of raw ambient and species-specific material collected during the trip, the best segments representing dawn, daytime, afternoon, dusk, evening, nighttime and pre-dawn were assembled. The most dramatic frogs, birds and mammals were tagged, and separated into short fragments that ranged in length from a few seconds to five minutes — some were near-field recordings, where the listener has a sense of being very close to the creatures vocalizing; some were far-field, others more distant.

These short segments were then copied to editing software, so that glitches and dropouts could be deleted and the strongest material retained. After editing, they were transferred to a multi-track analog tape machine with Dolby SR noise reduction, and mixed into longer segments. When these tapes were full, the longer elements were copied to a computer capable of handling and mixing up to 100 tracks of stereo information.

It's at this stage that all of the elements are given final, delicate calibration, and transformed into complete expressions of a theme. Care is taken to ensure that the stereo *imaging*—the way in which each creature is placed in the aural space of the recording—is dramatic, and that insects, birds and mammals appear to move naturally through the aural space. This is the most crucial component of the magic in any natural sound recording—without proper imaging sound becomes flat and uninteresting, the most formidable defect of most recordings on the market.

Lastly, a major part of the effort is knowing what creatures are featured, so that their effect can be maximized as part of the composition and an integrity of place maintained. For the record, *Amazon Days, Amazon Nights* took six months to mix.

A good example of the painstaking work required to create a "natural" recording is ocean sounds. Earlier, I alluded to what happens when we stand by the ocean shore, visualizing the wave action from different perspectives, with our brains adjusting what we hear to what's seen. The ocean album sample on this disk ("A Gift from the Sea") took over

100 hours of studio time and a mix of 60 digital stereo tracks before I felt I had created the sought-after sense of place. The same goes for mountain streams, for dawn or evening choruses in rain forests, and for river or desert habitats.

For a dozen years we couldn't figure out why these recordings never sounded right. At length this problem was resolved through better understanding of the medium, especially of microphones.

Microphones are able to pick out only the information within their given technical patterns, and are very limited. Our ears have the capacity to discriminate; microphones don't. Some gather sound narrowly, exactly where they are pointed—these are called "shotgun" mikes. Omni-directional microphones, on the other hand, pick up sound all around. (Various in-between types also exist.)

Because of the limitations of most consumer sound playback systems, the experience of environmental sound can't be reproduced by simply transferring field recordings unedited and unmixed to disk. Some producers, thinking that raw field recordings are more authentic, have attempted to sell their work as such—generally, such recordings are unevocative. (Listening carefully is, of course, a crucial part of the process.)

In the final analysis, the ways in which our original field recordings are transformed determines the aesthetic success of the material. Because the material is already changed by the process of field recording itself, and because the recorded sound is a mere fragment of the source material, the experience cannot be transferred to CD or other media without a strong awareness on the producer's part of the format's limitations. The raw material must be edited, mixed and remixed to create the illusion of reality.

Of course, various techniques are used. Some recordists prefer *binaural* techniques, which combine sound in somewhat the same way our ears do. This technique provides the listener with the illusion of having sound come from all around (up, down, from side to side, etc.). The problem for the listener is that a pair of stereo speakers will not reproduce this illusion. In order to achieve results from the technology, the listener has to remove him/herself still further from the natural environment by wearing earphones—even then, the listener will not be able to get the sense that sound is coming from a "front" perspective. I find this ridiculous.

The microphone system my collaborators and I choose is determined by how we plan to use the sounds. Some recordists prefer large parabolic dishes or shotgun mikes to capture specific birds, insects, amphibians or mammals. These systems, used mostly for scientific study of individual creature voices, tend to color sound too much for my taste—parabolic dishes, for example, make the sound thinner; and shotgun mikes add an unpleasant ring to some material. Most of my work is recorded in the field using "M-S" or "mid-side" technologies. Usually, I use two microphones, piggy-backed and recording simultaneously, to accomplish this. One mike—the mid mike—provides a very narrow pattern we use to gather species-specific sounds. The side mike provides a figure-eight pattern, so that while we are recording specific animals we're also recording their habitat. When we get back to the studio, we recombine the mid and side tracks for dramatic stereo results. We record in other formats as well, but prefer M-S because it gives us better imaging and depth. It also provides three results for the price of two: species-specific recordings from the mid mike, and/or ambiance from the side or figure eight mike, and/or stereo. This is useful to us when we analyze the effect of sound on a habitat, because we can work with only one or all of the components. In addition, we have to use mikes that won't fail in the high humidity of the rain forest and elsewhere. Every recorded example on the enclosed CD was recorded with M-S technology except—of course—our underwater recordings, which were done with hydrophones.

Aside from the quality of the field recordings themselves, we take care to learn what creatures we're recording. Although Harvard biologist E. O. Wilson has suggested scientists have identified less than five percent of the world's creatures, we do our best to convey what knowledge we have to the listener in our album notes.

We take care to insure the accuracy of our recordings. One label, eager to jump on the nature sound bandwagon in the late 80s, released an album of tropical Hawaiian sounds—or so the cover claimed. "Tropical birds" were allegedly the featured creatures. But the recordist didn't realize that the album's most prominently featured bird was the American finch commonly known as the cardinal, brought to Hawaii by nineteenth century missionaries so they could hear familiar bird song. This bird—among many creatures brought to paradise by missionaries—was so aggressive that it began replacing more gentle tropical avians. Thus began a cycle of destruction of island wildlife on a scale of magnitude unknown anywhere else on the planet. Today, less than one percent of Hawaii's original vegetation and wildlife is left. It's of no little consequence that the recordist in question got none of it. He was not a naturalist, and demonstrated no knowledge of what he recorded. Apparently, there was no one at the record company who knew, either. When this was pointed out to the company by a number of people, the president remarked that no one would notice. Be careful what you buy!

As for natural sound albums with music, when the music is derived from and inspired by natural sounds and the composer is sensitive to the impact natural sound has on orchestration, the result can be wonderful. As mentioned, the Pitjantjara, Bayaka and Jivaro hunter-gatherers still use forest sounds as a kind of natural *karaoke* to which they create their own complex poly-rhythmic and melodic music. Western composers can learn much by studying the relationship between the sounds of natural environments and the music of those who still live closely connected to them.

Last of all, the equipment to record need not be expensive and the experience of trying your hand at it is enlightening fun. Mostly, you'll learn just how much human noise pollution there is in your environment. Then you'll want to seek out quieter places. At that point we'll have become partners in the quest to hear more of the wonderful voices of the natural world.

Acknowledgments

This project could not have been completed without the help of my partner and wife, Katherine, who resorted to leaving food outside the door on those nights when I refused to stop working. She also offered many insightful suggestions when the manuscript became too obtuse. To my editor, Matt Kopka, who noted all the inconsistencies and wouldn't let them pass without change, and to the Ellipsis staff. To Doug Quin, who seems to be tireless in his pursuit of excellence. To Jeff Charno, the courageous one and true believer. To the late Loren Eiseley and Paul Shepard, whose writings continue to inspire me. To my father, who, in spite of his discomfort with the non-human world of living organisms, drove me to nearby farms on Sunday mornings so I could begin to experience "the others." And to the world's creatures, whose voices thankfully and forcefully remind us of our humble place in the universe.

Bernie Krause: Discography

Recordings:

*Nonesuch Guide to Electronic Music/*Nonesuch 1968*
Ragnarok (w/Paul Beaver)/*Limelite 1969*
In a Wild Sanctuary (w/Paul Beaver)/*Warner Brothers 1969*
Gandharva (w/Paul Beaver)/*Warner Brothers 1971*
All Good men (w/Paul Beaver)/*Warner Brothers 1973*
Citadels of Mystery/Takoma/*Mobile Fidelity 1979*
*Revised Nonesuch Guide to Electronic Music/*Nonesuch 1979*
Equator/*Nature Co. 1986*
Nature/*Nature Co. 1987*
Distant Thunder/*Nature Co. 1988*
Mountain Stream/*Nature Co. 1988*
Gentle Ocean/*Nature Co.*
Jungle Shoes/Fish Wra/*Rykodisk 1988*
Morning Song Birds/*Nature Co. 1988*
Sounds of a Summer's Evening/*Nature Co. 1988*
Tropical Rainforest/*Nature Co. 1989*
Gorilla/*Nature Co. 1989*
Gorillas in the Mix/*Rykodisk 1989*
Natural Voices/African Song Cycle/*Wild Sanctuary 1990*
Green Meadow Stream/*Wild Sanctuary 1990*
Woodland Journey/*Wild Sanctuary 1990*
Dawn at Trout Lake/*Wild Sanctuary 1990*
Meridian/*Nature Co.*
Amazon Days, Amazon Nights/*Wild Sanctuary 1990*
Ocean Wonders/*Wild Sanctuary 1991*
Nez Perce Stories/*Wild Sanctuary Word & Music 1991*
Music of the Nez Perce/*Wild Sanctuary Word & Music 1991*
Tropical Thunder/*Wild Sanctuary 1991*
Loons of Echo Pond**/*Wild Sanctuary 1991*
Wild Times at the Waterhole/*Wild Sanctuary Creatures 'n' Kids 1991*

Drums Across the Tundra/*Wild Sanctuary Word & Music 1992*
Ishi, the Last Yahi/*Wild Sanctuary Word & Music 1992*
Discover the Wonder (Grades 3-6)/*Scott Foresman*
Mata Atlantica (Atlantic Rainforest w/R. Happel)/*Wild Sanctuary 1994*
Desert Solitudes (w/Ruth Happel)/*Wild Sanctuary 1994*
Ocean Dreams/*Wild Sanctuary 1994*
Midsummer Nights (w/Ruth Happel)/*Wild Sanctuary 1994*
Nature's Lullabies (Wee Creatures Ages 1-3) Ocean, Rain, Stream/*Wild Sanctuary 1994*
African Adventures/*Wild Sanctuary 1994*
A Wild Christmas (w/Phil Aaberg)/*Wild Sanctuary 1994*
Whales, Wolves & Eagles of Glacier Bay/*Wild Sanctuary 1994*

*Standard reference

**Executive Producer

Public Space Installations

The California Academy of Sciences (San Francisco, CA)
African Waterhole Exhibit

The Aperture Foundation
Mountain Gorilla Touring Exhibit

St. Louis Zoo
Education Center

The Cleveland Zoo
RainForest Exhibit

Japanese-American National Museum (Los Angeles, CA)
The Issei Experience

Cranbrook School (Bloomfield Hills, MI)
Bat Exhibit

Smithsonian Institution (Washington, D.C.)
National Postal Museum

Rio Grande Zoo (Albuquerque, NM)
Nocturnal Exhibit

Houston Museum of Natural Science
Rainforest

Lisbon Aquarium
system design

Washington State Historical Museum (Tacoma, WA)
sound sculptures & interactive media

Mashantucket Pequot Museum (Ledyard, CT)
sound sculptures

Notes

[1] Formed in 1948, The Weavers were the most influential folk quartet America has produced. Their hits included "Good Night, Irene," "Guantanamera," "This Land is Your Land" and "If I Had A Hammer." Blacklisted during the 1950s for their political activism, they almost never had an opportunity to appear on television. Despite many setbacks, they thrived.

[2] Designed and built by Don Buchla (Berkeley, California) and Robert Moog (Trumansburg, NY) in 1963 and 1964, respectively.

[3] Beaver died in January 1975.

[4] With the introduction of the Ampex tape recorder in the late 40s, composers—among them Pierre Schaffer, Pierre Henry, Otto Luening and Vladimir Ussachevsky—began to experiment by splicing together short tape samples of ambient sound, most of them recorded in urban settings. These were edited—often by hand—into extended pieces of music called *musique concrète*. Our album, however, was the first to use extended recordings of natural sound and traditional Western instruments.

[5] Complete text of Chief Joseph's Carlisle Indian School 1904 speech: "I am very glad that I have children here from my tribe going to school to get an education; I am happy about it. It is good for them to get an education just as far as they can go. I am glad to see my children. Whenever I am back home again, I am going to encourage my children to get an education. I am glad that I am here with you. Here sits a man, Arm-Cut (Howard had lost an arm fighting in the Civil War, and this was how he was referred to by the Nez Perce). We were enemies at war and at that time I used to think I'd like to shoot and kill him and would have been happy over it. Today when we are old, he is my friend and I like him. I will never have anything against him again. Now our war is over."

CD Track Listing

1. Amazon Nights *(12:04)*
2. Desert Solitudes *(10:56)*
3. A Gift from the Sea *(12:16)*
4. Whales, Wolves and Eagles of Glacier Bay *(10:39)*
5. Gorillas in the Midst *(11:00)*
6. Green Meadow Stream *(10:36)*

Wild Sanctuary
13012 Henno Rd
Glen Ellen, CA 95442

Ph: 707-996-6677
Fax: 707-996-0280
WebPage: http://www.sonic.net/wildsanc/